BOURBON AT THE BORDER
BY PEARL CLEAGE

D1604092

DRAMATISTS
PLAY SERVICE
INC.

BOURBON AT THE BORDER
Copyright © 1997, 2005, Pearl Cleage

All Rights Reserved

SPECIAL NOTE

Commissioned by and World Premiere Presented at
ALLIANCE THEATRE COMPANY
Atlanta, Georgia

Artistic Director   Managing Director
Kenny Leon   Edith H. Love

SPECIAL NOTE ON SONGS AND RECORDINGS

2

AUTHOR'S NOTE

In the summer of 1964, the Student Nonviolent Coordinating Committee (SNCC), the Congress of Racial Equality (CORE), the Southern Christian Leadership Conference (SCLC), the Council of Federated Organizations (COFO), and the National Association for the Advancement of Colored People (NAACP) brought together grassroots organizers, students and movement veterans for a massive voter registration drive. The goal of the drive was the enfranchisement of thousands of Mississippi Negroes who had been systematically and violently denied their right to vote. The activists who went south called it the Mississippi Summer Project — Freedom Summer. Their experiences that summer — including the murders of Summer Project workers James Chancy, Andrew Goodman and Michael Schwerner, as well as the violence against many others whose names are unknown to us — exposed the level of American racial warfare in a way that was as dramatic as it was undeniable.

That same year, black playwright LeRoi Jones' *Dutchman* was produced in New York. The anguished assertion of Clay, the twenty-year-old Negro protagonist, that murder is the only solution to African-American madness is as real and as frightening now as it was then. Somewhere in the space between the nonviolent warriors and the powerless rage of the would-be poet, is the answer to the question W.E.B. Du Bois warned would shape the twentieth century: the question of the color line.

BOURBON AT THE BORDER was originally commissioned by The Alliance Theatre Company (Kenny Leon, Artistic Director; T. Jane Bishop, General Manager) in Atlanta, Georgia, where it premiered in 1997. It was directed by Kenny Leon; the set design was by Marjorie Bradley Kellogg; the costume design was by Susan E. Mickey; the lighting design was by Ann G. Wrightson; the sound design was by Brian Kettler; and the musical composition was by Dwight Andrews. The cast was as follows:

MAY THOMPSON .... Carol Mitchell-Leon
ROSA ST. JOHN .... Andrea Frye
CHARLES THOMPSON .... Terry Alexander
TYRONE WASHINGTON .... Taurean Blacque

CHARACTERS

MAY THOMPSON, an African-American woman, late 40s

ROSA ST. JOHN, an African-American woman, late 40s

CHARLES THOMPSON, an African-American man, late 40s

TYRONE WASHINGTON, an African-American man, late 40s

TIME

September 1995.

ACT ONE
Scene 1: Friday night
Scene 2: Saturday morning
Scene 3: Saturday night
Scene 4: Next Saturday

ACT TWO
Scene 1: Following Friday
Scene 2: Monday
Scene 3: Tuesday afternoon
Scene 4: Tuesday night

PLACE

Detroit, Michigan. All action takes place in May's apartment. There is a living area and a small kitchen separated from the larger room by a counter. There is also a door to an unseen bedroom. Located in an area of the city's downtown that is neither particularly fashionable nor particularly safe, the apartment's most striking feature is its view of the Ambassador Bridge connecting Detroit to Windsor, Ontario, Canada. On clear days and at night, when it is lit, the bridge is almost a presence in the apartment.

BOURBON AT THE BORDER

ACT ONE

Scene 1

May's apartment. Friday, early evening. The apartment is already neat as a pin, but May is nervously plumping pillows, straightening pictures, slightly altering one chair or another. She surveys her work and, finally satisfied, sits down, picks up a magazine, flips through it, puts it down, gets up, paces, sits again, picks up an envelope, withdraws several snapshots, looks at them as if searching for the answer to a familiar question. The doorbell rings. Although this is what she's been waiting for, she takes a moment to gather herself together, then goes to the door and opens it quickly. Rosa St. John is standing there. She is dressed to the nines — high heels, full makeup, after-five dress. Rosa sweeps into the apartment and strikes a pose in the middle of the room.

ROSA. Well?

MAY. I thought you were going out.

ROSA. I am. Tell me the truth.

MAY. About what?

ROSA. This outfit! I got it at the resale shop but you know how little that dressing room is down there, if you can even call it that, and Doris will tell you anything makes you look like Miss Black America if you give her five dollars for it! I think she purposely angles that mirror so you can't see your behind!

MAY. It looks great on you.

ROSA. I know that, but is it, you know …

MAY. What?

ROSA. Is it too young for me?

MAY. How young is too young?

ROSA. Tyrone thinks I'm forty-five …

MAY. You told him you were forty-five!

ROSA. That is neither here nor there. The point is, the only way to pull off forty-five is not to go overboard and start pretending thirty-five. *(Rosa is vain, but insecure about her looks at this age. Throughout this scene, she fixes her makeup, applies more lipstick and fusses with her dress.)*

MAY. How old is he?

ROSA. He ain't no child, but it's different for men.

MAY. Why is that?

ROSA. Because they make the rules.

MAY. Then why don't you tell him the truth?

ROSA. Oh, sure. That would be a great way to start the evening: "Hey, baby! Guess what?" I don't think so.

MAY. What do you always tell me?

ROSA. What?

MAY. Age ain't nothin' but a number.

ROSA. I don't know why I'm even asking you. It's been so long since you went out, you don't have anything to compare it to.

MAY. I'm out all the time!

ROSA. Going to work does not count.

MAY. You look beautiful. Tyrone won't know what hit him.

ROSA. He's already seen it.

MAY. What did he say?

ROSA. *(Grinning.)* He said I looked good enough to eat.

MAY. Then what are you doing down here harassing me?

ROSA. Trying to get a second opinion. You know men will tell you anything when they want something.

MAY. What time is the show?

ROSA. Eight o'clock, but Tyrone wants to get there early so we can park close to the club. I told him if he's so worried about that Cadillac, he needs to go on and get him an old raggedy Ford so he can relax.

MAY. Where is he?

ROSA. He went to the liquor store. I told him I had to finish fixing my face and to pick me up down here.

MAY. Oh. Well …

ROSA. Am I interrupting something?

MAY. No, I was just thinking I might be going out in a minute, too ...

ROSA. *(Immediately suspicious.)* Going out where?

MAY. I don't have to get your permission, do I?

ROSA. Hell no, honey! I've been trying to get you outta here for months. *(A beat.)* You got a date?

MAY. Of course not!

ROSA. Don't say of course not. Charlie's been gone almost all summer.

MAY. He's coming home.

ROSA. Sure he is, honey, but you're only human and when the cat's away, who knows what the mice might do?

MAY. He's coming home today.

ROSA. Today?

MAY. I thought it was him when you rang the bell.

ROSA. Why didn't you tell me?

MAY. I know how you feel about all this ...

ROSA. You're not picking him up?

MAY. He asked me not to.

ROSA. Then who's bringing him?

MAY. He's on the bus.

ROSA. The bus?

MAY. He said if he can't get home by himself, he doesn't need to be out.

ROSA. I heard that.

MAY. But he should be here by now.

ROSA. Don't worry. He can find this place in his sleep.

MAY. I guess you're right.

ROSA. I'm always right. *(A beat.)* May?

MAY. Yeah?

ROSA. Don't get mad when I say this, but it might be good for us to wait with you until he gets here.

MAY. Why?

ROSA. To make sure he's ... okay.

MAY. *(Sharply.)* He's coming home, isn't he?

ROSA. They sent him home last time, too, and said he was fine. Next thing you know he's back up on the roof. *(A beat.)*

MAY. Maybe you should wait for Tyrone upstairs.

ROSA. You don't have to put me out, honey. I'll give you my opinion all day and all night, but once you make your choice, I'm on

9

your side. Whichever way it comes out.

MAY. I know. I didn't mean to snap at you.

ROSA. Are you nervous?

MAY. A little. It's just sort of sudden, you know? He hadn't been doing good at all. I couldn't get him to talk to me. Sometimes I wasn't even sure he knew I was there. It was like he was going in deeper and deeper and there wasn't any way to make him come back. I kept trying to get the doctor to tell me something, but they didn't know anything either. They kept on asking me what did I think had set him off this time and I kept on telling them if I knew what set him off, I'd know how to keep him away from it!

ROSA. Why they asking you? I thought you were paying them every dime you got to figure it out.

MAY. I told them that, too. But then about a month ago, he changed. He started talking and laughing again. He took the medicine they wanted him to try on the schedule they gave him. When I went to see him last time, he even —

ROSA. What? He even what?

MAY. He was flirting with me.

ROSA. In the hospital?

MAY. Well, it's not like he's in bed with one of those ass-out gowns on. We're in a regular room, sitting on a couch, talking like regular people.

ROSA. They let you be alone with him?

MAY. He's not dangerous, Rose. The only person he ever tries to hurt is himself.

ROSA. What did he say?

MAY. He said he had figured it out and he was going to be a new man. He said he was going to come home and get a job and make up for everything.

ROSA. (Skeptical.) He's going to be a making up something if you ask me.

MAY. Be glad for me, Rose.

ROSA. I am glad, honey. I'm real glad. I just don't want you to get all worked up before you have a chance to talk to him. You know. See how he's really doing.

MAY. He said I embarrassed him last time I picked him up.

ROSA. You didn't act a fool up in the place, did you?

MAY. I couldn't help it! I was doing fine until he walked in the room and then I just … I just felt like if I couldn't touch him, I'd go crazy.

ROSA. Don't do that! One to a family is all that's allowed. (A

10

beat.) I'm sorry. I didn't mean that the way it sounded.

MAY. How did you mean it?

ROSA. I meant to say good for you and good for Charlie and I hope by the time he gets here I'll have a chance to get my foot out of my mouth long enough to say welcome home. *(A beat.)* Don't be mad, honey. If I didn't say the wrong thing, I probably wouldn't say nothin' at all.

MAY. The truth of it is, I could use a little company. I've been up since six and if I pick up that magazine one more time, I'll know it by heart!

ROSA. Maybe he'll get here before we leave and we can pinch enough bourbon off Ty for a welcome-home toast.

MAY. I don't know, Rose. He might not be in the mood for company right at first.

ROSA. Just one? For the fellowship?

MAY. I guess one would be okay.

ROSA. That's all you gonna get, trust me. Tyrone got plenty of money, but he's stingy as the day is long. You know why he went to the liquor store?

MAY. To buy liquor?

ROSA. Of course to buy liquor, but why?

MAY. Why?

ROSA. When we first get to the club, he orders two bourbon and cokes, right?

MAY. Right …

ROSA. After that, all he'll order is plain Cokes and we gotta sneak and add the taste to it from the bottle we brought in with us.

MAY. You're kidding.

ROSA. I wish I was. Last time he spilled Jack Daniels all over me trying to pour it under the table. You remember that white linen skirt I got from Doris? Stain never did come out. This time, I'm pouring. He ain't messin' up another dress of mine with his cheap self. Speaking of cheap, what you got I can nibble on real quick? I know Ty ain't thinking about feeding me.

MAY. I got some tuna fish in there.

ROSA. To be working in a cafeteria, you got the sorriest refrigerator of anybody I know.

MAY. They don't pay me in food.

ROSA. I know that, but even when I used to work in people's houses, we got to take the leftovers home.

MAY. Take it or leave it.

ROSA. Never mind. I won't be thinking about food once the show starts anyway. Johnny Taylor in a club that size? I'm going to lose my mind!

MAY. Won't Tyrone get jealous?

ROSA. He better! That's the whole point. *(Suddenly.)* Sh-h-h!

MAY. *(Instantly quiet and on the alert.)* What?

ROSA. Don't you hear that?

MAY. Hear what?

ROSA. My stomach is growling so loud I won't be able to hear the music! Is it too late for me to change my mind about that tuna?

MAY. I'll make you a sandwich. *(She does as they talk.)*

ROSA. Don't put mayonnaise on it. I hate mayonnaise on a tuna sandwich! Guess what? My brother, the one who lives in Chicago? He called and said it snowed last night! Just barely September and they had snow! I don't see how anybody can live there. Detroit is as cold as I can stand.

MAY. My first winter up here, I almost froze to death. Charlie kept bringing me coats and sweaters, but I couldn't get warm no matter what I put on.

ROSA. When I was a kid, it used to be so cold on Halloween you'd have to wear your coat over your costume and when people opened the door for trick or treat, you'd flash 'em fast so you didn't get pneumonia.

MAY. First snow I saw was out this window. Charlie was sleep and I came out the bedroom and saw it. One of those wet, heavy snows, coming down thick. I screamed so loud, I probably woke up the whole building.

ROSA. What were you screaming about? Snow ain't never hurt nobody who wasn't out in it without enough clothes on.

MAY. I don't know. It surprised me, I guess. Just to see it coming down like that and not making a bit of noise. Like if I hadn't gotten up, I never would have known it was there at all.

ROSA. You'd know when you went out to start your car and had to spend ten minutes scraping it off the windows.

MAY. I kind of like it now. It's peaceful.

ROSA. May?

MAY. Yeah?

ROSA. You know I didn't mean anything before about Charlie. I just meant, you know, I've been living here five years and he's been in more than he's been out.

MAY. He's not dangerous, Rose. He's depressed.

ROSA. A lot of people get depressed from time to time, but Charlie is the first black person I ever knew who went all the way crazy.

MAY. Me, too.

ROSA. For real? Was it weird?

MAY. Was what weird?

ROSA. When you found out he was really crazy.

MAY. By the time I had to put a word on it, I think I already knew.

ROSA. Most folks wouldn't a stuck like you have.

MAY. Most folks won't stick if you have cancer either.

ROSA. That's different.

MAY. Why? He didn't get sick on purpose. He just got sick. *(A beat.)* I wish you could have seen him before. You would have liked him.

ROSA. I like him now! *(May picks up the envelope she put aside earlier, withdraws the snapshots, hands one to Rosa.)*

MAY. Recognize any of these bright-eyed, young Negroes?

ROSA. Oh, my God! Is that you?

MAY. Me and Charlie in our prime. I got a letter from my sister today. She found these in Mama's closet and sent them on.

ROSA. Look at all that hair on your head!

MAY. Going natural was supposed to set us free, but I spent as much time braiding and blowing out and Afro-picking as I ever did trying to keep a perm together.

ROSA. You all look so serious.

MAY. We were serious.

ROSA. You really got into that sixties thing, didn't you?

MAY. That's why I went to Howard in the first place. *(A beat.)* Look at Charlie. He was the main one talking people into going to Mississippi. Every day at noon, he'd be standing down there on the steps of Douglass Hall, talking about how we'd be the sorriest people on the face of this earth if we let a bunch of white kids go down there to register all those black folks to vote.

ROSA. Old Charlie was fine, too!

MAY. One day I stopped to listen and when he started up on how it wouldn't be fair for us to let these white kids fight our battles for us, I said, trying to be funny, fair to who? A couple of people standing around laughed, but Charlie looked at me real serious and said, fair to the memory of our ancestors' bones.

ROSA. Damn!

MAY. That made me feel guilty as hell, of course, so I stayed around to apologize and he asked me to go for coffee.

ROSA. And the rest is history.

MAY. I don't know about all that, but I kept trying to apologize and he kept trying to ask me if I didn't want to be a part of changing how the world worked. Finally, I said, look, I can think of more interesting ways to spend my summer than trudging around Mississippi trying to register some scared Negroes to vote, and he gave me that look again. Next thing I knew, I was on the bus to Sunflower County.

ROSA. Did you already know you were in love with him?

MAY. I followed him to Mississippi. How much more proof can you stand?

ROSA. Who is this?

MAY. Those are the Hemphills, the family I stayed with.

ROSA. What do you mean stayed with?

MAY. We all stayed with families. It broke down all that stuff about them being poor and ignorant and us being missionaries coming to save them.

ROSA. This whole family in that one little house?

MAY. You could stand at the front door and see clear through to the back porch. Neat as a pin. They had nine kids and almost no money, but they took me in like I was family. See this girl?

ROSA. The one holding the baby?

MAY. That's Esther and that's her little brother, John F. Kennedy Hemphill, also known as Prez. She was the oldest and she was seriously in love with a big old country boy from down the road about six miles. They both had to work the fields every day but he always came to walk her to church on Sunday. She'd wake up real early to get eveybody fed, then she'd put on her one good dress and sit down on the front porch to watch for him coming up that road. I sat with her sometimes and I swear, I've never seen anybody in love like that in my life. When he came around that bend, she'd catch her breath like Jesus Christ himself was walking up that road.

ROSA. Maybe it was like those stories where Jesus is there in a regular place, looking like a regular person, so nobody knows it's him until most of them have treated him like a dog and then they all feel ashamed, but it's too late and only the ones who were nice to him get to go to heaven.

MAY. Well, if this boy was the baby Jesus in disguise, Esther Hemphill is guaranteed a place at the right hand of God.

ROSA. *(Picking up a yellowed clipping.)* "Three Civil Rights Workers Missing, Feared Dead." Did you know them?

MAY. No. We were still in training. Up in Ohio, thinking we were going down there and they were going to roll over and play dead. My grandmother called me and started crying and begging me not to go. *(A beat.)* Part of what made it so hard was that they were missing for weeks. Even after we got there, we'd be driving around, walking around, wondering if this one or that one was the killer. We knew they were dead. We weren't that naive. It was pretty scary. Some people couldn't take it. They got too scared to function.

ROSA. What happened to them?

MAY. They went home.

ROSA. But you stayed.

MAY. As long as we could, then Charlie got hurt and we came up here.

ROSA. What's this woman so mad about? Look how she's looking at that guy.

MAY. That's her husband. He had finally agreed to come down to the courthouse to register. We were so proud and he was so proud. All of his kids were excited, but his wife knew that if he really did it, there was a good chance they'd lose the little bit they had. We kept on talking about how proud her sons were going to be, but she wasn't buying it. Then, all of a sudden, he said he was tired of being scared and if the white folks were going to do something to him, they were going to have to just go ahead and do it. *(A beat.)* That's the first time somebody followed us. When we left that place.

ROSA. Followed you?

MAY. A car full of young white boys saw us turn out of the plantation road and fell in behind us. People told us the best thing to do was head for town as fast as you could since they were less likely to act a fool if other folks were around, so I hit the gas. Those Mississippi back roads were pitch-black at night. We had only been driving them a couple of weeks, but I was taking those curves at sixty miles an hour.

ROSA. Were you scared?

MAY. Sure I was. They hugged our bumper the whole way back to town. Sometimes we could hear them laughing and hollering out the window. There had to be five or six of them. Once we hit town, they just turned off. I was shaking so bad when we finally got back to where we were staying, it was a shame. Charlie was trying to act brave so I wouldn't know how scared he was, but I could see it on his face. I was about ready to go home that night, but it was too late to start out anywhere, so we sat up talking. Trying to understand. By morning, it almost seemed like it had happened to somebody else, so we got up and went back to work.

ROSA. Do you ever wish you hadn't gone down there at all?

MAY. Never. *(The doorbell rings. Rosa starts for the door, but May stops her.)* I'll get it. *(May opens the door to Tyrone.)*

TYRONE. Greetings and salutations! Is there a blues-lovin' woman on the premises who's looking for a blues-lovin' man?

ROSA. You got that right!

TYRONE. How you doin', May?

MAY. I'm good, Tyrone. You?

TYRONE. Couldn't be better. I got a brand-new Cadillac, a pocket full of money and a fine woman who likes to call me "sweet thing."

ROSA. Not necessarily in that order.

TYRONE. Let's hit the street, babe. You know those Negroes will have double-parked all the good spaces by seven-thirty!

ROSA. We got time. Guess what?

TYRONE. What?

ROSA. Charlie's coming home today.

TYRONE. Who?

MAY. My husband, Charlie.

ROSA. You know I told you about Charlie.

TYRONE. *(He clearly doesn't remember.)* Oh, right! Where's he been?

MAY. In the hospital.

TYRONE. Yeah? What happened?

MAY. He got hurt in Mississippi a long time ago.

TYRONE. Mississippi?

ROSA. Charlie and May were in the civil rights movement.

TYRONE. What happened?

MAY. Freedom Summer. You ever heard of it?

TYRONE. The sixties, right?

MAY. Sixty-four.

TYRONE. I always thought those Negroes were crazy going down there.

MAY. It wasn't that big a leap for me. I was born in Georgia.

TYRONE. That's why you still got that little Southern sweetness in your voice. Every girl I meet from down home sound like she been suckin' on a sugar tit.

ROSA. Tyrone! Be nice!

TYRONE. I didn't mean nothin'.

ROSA. Gentlemen do not use that word in mixed company.

TYRONE. "Tit" ain't necessarily a bad word. Depends on how you use it. All I was doin' was callin' it what they call it. No offense, May.

MAY. It's okay.

TYRONE. Where in Georgia you from?

MAY. Near Madison. It's about an hour outside of Atlanta.

TYRONE. *(Laughs.)* Well, a miss is as good as a mile!

ROSA. Everybody ain't from the city like you, sweet thing.

TYRONE. Say it again.

ROSA. *(Suggestively.)* Sweet thing.

TYRONE. If I hadn't paid for these tickets in advance, I'd toss them out the window and take you back upstairs right now!

ROSA. You gonna get your money's worth all the way around. Trust me.

TYRONE. Well, I don't trust nobody to hold back time and I ain't up for fighting about no parking space.

ROSA. Did you get the bourbon?

TYRONE. *(He takes a pint bottle from his pocket.)* Mr. Jack Black, present and accounted for!

ROSA. Listen, Ty, I'd love for you to have a chance to meet Charlie before we go.

TYRONE. When's he coming?

MAY. He's on his way.

TYRONE. We ain't got time for all that now, Rosa.

ROSA. Then how about the three of us have a quick drink and May can tell Brother Charles we toasted him in absentia?

TYRONE. That ain't what I bought it for, whatever that means.

MAY. Maybe we should do this another time.

ROSA. When? *(She goes to the kitchen and gets four glasses.)* Charlie's coming home today. If we don't do it now, it'll be bad luck to double back and try to catch up later.

TYRONE. Be bad luck to run outta booze before the second show. *(A beat.)*

ROSA. I would hate to think our whole evening could be ruined over a couple a shots of liquor among friends.

TYRONE. All right, all right. *(He carefully pours three tiny shots.)*

ROSA. Put some in Charlie's glass, too.

TYRONE. He ain't even here!

ROSA. It's symbolic, honey. Like communion. *(Tyrone reluctantly pours an even smaller shot in the remaining empty glass. To Charlie.)*

MAY. To Charlie. *(A beat.)*

TYRONE. To Charlie. *(They drink.)*

ROSA. And now, before we make our exit, in plenty of time, I have a new joke.

MAY. No, Rose!

TYRONE. We gotta go, baby.

ROSA. It's a knock-knock joke.

MAY. I'm not doing it.

ROSA. It's a short knock-knock joke.

MAY. You can't tell jokes!

ROSA. This one is so easy even I won't mess it up. Come on, Ty, please?

TYRONE. Okay. Go ahead.

ROSA. Knock-knock.

TYRONE. Who's there?

ROSA. Banana.

TYRONE. Banana who?

ROSA. Knock-knock.

TYRONE. You already said that.

ROSA. I know, but I have to say it again. That's part of the joke.

TYRONE. Oh.

MAY. Don't look at me. I'm not in it.

ROSA. So you have to answer again, too.

TYRONE. Oh. *(Clearly confused.)* What is it?

ROSA. Knock-knock.

TYRONE. Who's there?

ROSA. Banana.

TYRONE. Banana who?

ROSA. Knock-knock.

MAY. Rosa!

ROSA. This is the end part! Just one more. Knock-knock.

TYRONE. *(Exasperated.)* Maybe we should just catch a cab 'cause there will be no place to park.

MAY. Who's there?

ROSA. Orange.

MAY. Orange who?

ROSA. Orange you glad I didn't say banana? *(Tyrone laughs. May groans.)*

TYRONE. Now can we go?

ROSA. Yes! Now we can go.

TYRONE. Nothing against you about the liquor, May. It's just that I'm watching my money pretty close these days. I'm getting ready to make some moves and I gotta bring some to get some, you know what I mean?

MAY. Sure, Ty. No problem. *(Tyrone turns to go and sees Rosa looking at him disapprovingly. A beat.)*

18

TYRONE. Ah, what the hell! *(He gives May the rest of the bourbon.)* Tell your old man I said welcome home.

MAY. You don't have to do that.

TYRONE. What's a pint among friends?

ROSA. You sweet thing! *(She kisses him.)* Drinks at the club are on me!

TYRONE. *(Grinning.)* Say it again.

ROSA. Sweet thing.

TYRONE. No, I mean the part about who's buying the drinks!

ROSA. Call me in the morning.

MAY. I will.

TYRONE. Okay, okay! Let's get a move on else we gonna have to park in Cincinnati! *(Tyrone and Rosa exit. May closes the door, clears away the glasses and the bourbon. Now that Tyrone and Rosa are gone, she is again left with nothing to do but wait. She goes to the window and stands looking out. As she watches, the bridge lights are illuminated for the night. Time passes. The sound of a key in the lock as Charlie enters. He has a slight limp. May stands, but does not move toward him. He closes the door, but does not move toward her. They stand looking at each other for a beat. Although they will not touch each other until the end of this scene, it is obvious that they are longing to do so from the time he enters.)*

CHARLIE. Hello, May.

MAY. Hello, Charlie.

CHARLIE. I didn't mean to worry you.

MAY. Are you all right?

CHARLIE. Yes.

MAY. It got so late.

CHARLIE. I figured it out, May. The only way they win is if they make me too crazy to be with you.

MAY. Oh, Charlie. *(May begins to cry. He embraces and caresses her.)*

CHARLIE. Don't cry, baby. It's over now. It's all over. Daddy's home. Daddy's home … *(May returns his caresses as the lights fade to black.)*

Scene 2

The next morning. Charlie, fully dressed, is up drinking a cup of coffee and looking out the window. May comes out of the bedroom wearing a robe. Her manner is casual, but she is completely focused on getting a clear reading on Charlie's mental state. There is between them an intangible but undeniable air of desire unfulfilled.

MAY. I didn't hear you get up.
CHARLIE. You weren't supposed to. *(She joins him at the window.)*
MAY. You sleep all right?
CHARLIE. Like a baby. You?
MAY. Yeah, until you woke me up with those big old cold feet!
CHARLIE. Tonight I'll wear socks.
MAY. That's all right. Once I was awake, I had a chance to take a look at you without you knowing it.
CHARLIE. Did I pass inspection?
MAY. So far, so good.
CHARLIE. Maybe we can ride over to Canada next weekend and get a cabin for a couple of days so you can complete your examination.
MAY. Let's do it today.
CHARLIE. Can't do it today. I gotta go over to Northland. They're hiring at Hudson's warehouse. *(A beat.)*
MAY. You don't have to do that.
CHARLIE. Yes I do.
MAY. Why don't you wait until Monday?
CHARLIE. What's going to happen between now and then, do you think?
MAY. You'll have a chance to rest.
CHARLIE. I've been resting.
MAY. I think the warehouse is a bad idea.
CHARLIE. I've only got a couple of choices. I can sit here and let you take care of me because I'm too crazy to be moving around out in the world, or I can get off my black, insane ass and figure out how to take care of my wife like a man is supposed to do.
MAY. Who gets to decide what a man is supposed to do?

CHARLIE. Only the man in question, otherwise it's all bullshit. I gotta get a job, May. I can't let you talk me out of it for my own good.

MAY. What did the doctor say?

CHARLIE. The doctor said I'm no crazier than most of the folks walking around out here and they're doing fine. Plus, I've got lots of new medication. I've got pills for when I get up in the morning and pills for when I go to bed at night. I've got pills that can chase the blues and pills to soothe the savage beast. Stop worrying.

MAY. Did he say anything about whether or not you should be working?

CHARLIE. Listen, May. Three weeks ago, they put me in with a new doctor. I'm not making much progress but they think maybe I'll do better with this guy than I'm doing with the other one. So I'm sitting in the office, talking to him and he's an Indian, an India Indian, not a Native American brother, and he was asking me questions and scribbling down notes when I answered, I mean lots of notes, like everything I said was critical to him understanding my problem, whatever they had told him my problem was. And I'm thinking to myself, this guy is really taking this serious. Maybe he can help me figure this stuff out, even if he is an Indian. I mean, I'm damn near fifty years old. Time should be on my side, right? And I been in a lot of shrinks' offices and I don't remember one of them writing down a single word. Then the guy got an emergency phone call and practically broke his neck running out to take it, but he left that pad, so I went over and picked it up to see what he'd been writing about me and it said: "My darling, please forgive me for what I've done. I love only you and always will. Please, my angel, can't we start again?" He wasn't writing about me at all. He wasn't even thinking about me. He was trying to beg some woman for her forgiveness and that was more important than anything I had to say. And you know what? It didn't even make me mad. It was like a sign or something. A sign to me about what's really important. About love and how easy you can fuck it up by being too selfish or too mean or too crazy to see the cure is standing right beside you. *(A beat.)*

MAY. At first, when they wouldn't let me in to see you, I'd drive out there anyway and make them tell me no every day like I didn't remember what they said the day before. Then I'd go walk around outside the building for an hour as close as I could get so maybe you would pass by a window and see me.

CHARLIE. *(Quietly.)* There were no windows ...

21

MAY. No windows?

CHARLIE. Not at first.

MAY. *(Quickly recovering.)* I always wore that dress you like.

CHARLIE. The green one?

MAY. *(Quoting him.)* The one that floats on me like water ...

CHARLIE. Did you have the hat?

MAY. Yes.

CHARLIE. And those shoes with the high heels?

MAY. You sure you didn't see me?

CHARLIE. I felt you.

MAY. Promise me something?

CHARLIE. What's that?

MAY. If the foreman has a Confederate flag in his office, on his cap or anywhere on his person, you won't take the job.

CHARLIE. I promise!

MAY. Do you really have to go?

CHARLIE. Yes! I won't be late. Even if I get it, they won't start me today.

MAY. I love you, Charlie. *(Charlie closes his eyes, puts one hand over his heart, sighs dramatically, grins, blows May a kiss and exits. Phone rings.)* Hello? Hey, Rose. Yeah. Last night. He's gone out. Where's Ty? Sure, come on down. *(May makes more coffee. Rosa rings the bell almost immediately.)*

ROSA. I thought you were going to call me.

MAY. Charlie just left a minute ago. I'm surprised you didn't see him in the hall.

ROSA. I wasn't sure if you had left a message and I never play them back when Ty stays over. All I need is for some old fool to resurface feeling frisky and leave me a message for old time's sake.

MAY. You ought to quit!

ROSA. So where is he?

MAY. He went out to look for work.

ROSA. *(Surprised.)* On Saturday morning?

MAY. He said they're hiring at Hudson's warehouse. Just until he can find something better.

ROSA. I saw that Hudson's notice in the paper yesterday, too. I started to go down there myself.

MAY. To the warehouse?

ROSA. Sonny's insurance ain't going as far as I hoped it would, rest in peace, and me and Tyrone drank up half my savings at the club last night. Now I know why he's always sneaking something in. Five dollars for bourbon and coke! And it's a crime what they're charging for a shot of cognac!

MAY. How was the show?

ROSA. Girl, don't get me started! We were so close when he started singing "Disco Lady," I could see the sweat pop out on his face. And guess what?

MAY. I'm scared to.

ROSA. When he sang "I Believe in You," he came over and picked up my hand and started singing it straight to me. I almost passed out.

MAY. That was probably all the expensive bourbon you were drinking.

ROSA. I swear that Negro is so fine if I'd a been by myself he'd a had a helluva time getting rid of me. But enough about my night. What time did Brother Charles finally make his appearance?

MAY. Not long after you left.

ROSA. And?

MAY. And what?

ROSA. So how is he?

MAY. He's fine.

ROSA. That's it? He's fine?

MAY. That's it. He's fine. *(A beat.)*

ROSA. Do they think he'll try it again? *(A beat.)*

MAY. He won't try it again.

ROSA. How do you know?

MAY. *(Sharply.)* Because I won't let him. *(A beat.)* Want some coffee?

ROSA. Sure. *(A brief silence. Rosa cannot think of a way to get May to talk about Charlie, so she abandons the effort for the moment.)* You hear what happened?

MAY. What?

ROSA. They found a body downtown.

MAY. A body? Where?

ROSA. Right near the park.

MAY. No kidding? What happened?

ROSA. They don't know. No motive. No suspects.

MAY. Probably some more gang stuff.

ROSA. Not hardly. This was a white guy.

MAY. Really?

ROSA. An old white guy. Still had his wallet and his car keys on him.

MAY. What was he doing downtown?

ROSA. They still do business around here.

MAY. Not after this they won't.

ROSA. The cops are going to arrest everybody they even think might have done it.

MAY. All the men living in that park, they ought to have a field day.

ROSA. Tyrone said for me to be careful walking around by myself.

MAY. He's right.

ROSA. I'm always careful. I been running these streets all my life and I'm not about to quit now.

MAY. It's going to get worse before it gets better.

ROSA. You sound like that guy preaching in front of the grocery store. "There will be wars and rumors of wars."

MAY. I don't know about all that, but me and Charlie are not going to stick around for it, whatever it's going to be.

ROSA. Where are you going?

MAY. We're moving to Canada.

ROSA. To live?

MAY. Soon as I can talk Charlie into it.

ROSA. Have you ever been there?

MAY. It's right across the bridge. Haven't you?

ROSA. I went a couple of times, but what's the point, you know? Windsor ain't that much different from Detroit if you ask me.

MAY. It's different if you go out in the country.

ROSA. You moving to the woods?

MAY. Don't say it like that. It's beautiful.

ROSA. I can just see you and Charlie out there for about two weeks, then you'd come running back to the good old USA.

MAY. Not a chance. Charlie's different over there. One time we rented cabin. We woke up in the morning and there was so much snow we couldn't hardly see the car. The sun was out and the air was so clean you wanted to drink it like water. You'll have to come and visit us. Tyrone can come, too.

ROSA. Tyrone ain't hardly interested in no weekend in the woods.

MAY. You'd be surprised how different a man will act out in nature.

ROSA. Different how?

MAY. It brings out something good in them. Being in nature, knowing they're connected to something bigger.

ROSA. Bigger than what?

MAY. Say what you want, you'll be knocking on our door when the city gets too crazy to live in.

ROSA. It's already too crazy to live in, so what can you do?

MAY. You weren't really thinking about going down to the warehouse, were you?

ROSA. I surely was. Once I pay my rent and buy a couple bags of groceries, I'm all in.

MAY. They're hiring at the city.

ROSA. In the cafeteria?

MAY. No, night work.

ROSA. Night work doing what?

MAY. Clean-up or security.

ROSA. I am not hardly ready to start scrubbing floors and you know I ain't shooting nobody over something that don't even belong to me!

MAY. Suit yourself.

ROSA. If I tell you something, will you promise not to tell Tyrone?

MAY. What is it?

ROSA. You have to promise!

MAY. I promise.

ROSA. I interviewed for a phone sex job.

MAY. What?!

ROSA. Don't sound so shocked. You don't actually do anything. You just talk about it.

MAY. What did you say?

ROSA. Well, first they asked me if I had any hang-ups about any-thing. I said not as far as I know, then the guy started asking me —

MAY. A man interviewed you?

ROSA. He owns the place.

MAY. Go on ...

ROSA. He asked me if I had ever faked an orgasm.

MAY. What'd you tell him?

ROSA. I told him no! *(May raises her eyebrows.)* Force of habit, okay? But I told him I was sure I could do it, so he started asking me about specific stuff and, girl, I swear, it was all I could do to keep from putting my fingers in my ears and running out the place.

MAY. Stuff like what?

ROSA. You know, animals and stuff.

MAY. Animals?

ROSA. It's a big world, honey. Everybody got a right to do their own thing.

MAY. Yeah, but animals?

ROSA. Don't worry. I told him I didn't know nothing about no animals and he said that was fine. They didn't get much call for that during the day anyway — I told him I could only work in the daytime — and how did I feel about S and M?

MAY. Did you tell him you were a Baptist?

ROSA. I told him I was a meat and potatoes kind of gal and if they specialized in all that freaky-deaky stuff I should probably take my business elsewhere.

MAY. Good for you!

ROSA. So he said everything was fine and asked me if I'd do an audition.

MAY. I thought you said it was just on the phone.

ROSA. It is, but you still got to audition. They aren't going to hook you up with a paying customer if you can't come through, no pun intended.

MAY. So what did you do?

ROSA. He put me in this little cubicle, like a telephone operator, you know, and then he called me up.

MAY. Jesus, Rose! Weren't you embarrassed?

ROSA. I'm too broke to be embarrassed.

MAY. What did he say?

ROSA. Nothing too weird, you know, he would tell me what he was gonna do to me and I had to moan and groan and act like it was driving me crazy to hear about it and then he started breathing real hard so I started breathing real hard and that was about it.

MAY. I can just hear you huffin' and puffin'. "I think I can! I think I can!"

ROSA. I know I can! I even hollered a little at the end.

MAY. I can't believe you did this.

ROSA. You know guys like it when you scream. Makes them feel like they got you to give up something you been holding back.

MAY. Are you going to take the job?

ROSA. I told him I had to think about it. He told me I was a natural.

MAY. A natural what?

ROSA. Whatever! The weirdest part about it was — don't laugh! — I really got into it.

MAY. I don't want to hear this.

ROSA. It was like dancing or something. All I had to do was follow his lead.

MAY. I think you can do better.

ROSA. Yeah, how? Sweeping up at City Hall after you unionized day workers have gone home?

MAY. Clean-up isn't so bad. At least it's quiet and you get to work by yourself.

ROSA. I don't see you running down to apply for the job.

MAY. I already did.

ROSA. Did what?

MAY. Applied for night crew. I been working three nights a week all summer. With Charlie being away, I needed something to do and we can use the extra money.

ROSA. I ain't never loved no man enough to work two jobs for him.

MAY. It won't be long. Soon as Charlie gets something, I'll quit.

ROSA. You want me to ask this guy at the sex shop if he's got another opening?

MAY. No, thanks. I couldn't do that.

ROSA. You too high-class to fake it?

MAY. It's not that. I just think some things are private.

ROSA. You're a romantic, May. You know that? All for love!

MAY. That's not a bad thing, is it?

ROSA. No. It's kind of sweet actually. Impractical, but kind of sweet. I don't think I ever felt that way.

MAY. Not even about Sonny?

ROSA. Maybe at the beginning, but not enough to be scrubbing no floors to prove it.

MAY. *(Defensive.)* I'm not proving anything.

ROSA. Then what are you — May! I've got a proposition for you.

MAY. I'm fine, really.

ROSA. Charlie's looking for a job, right?

MAY. Right.

ROSA. And the doctor says it's okay, right?

MAY. Right.

ROSA. Well, last night, Ty was talking about how his boss was looking for a couple of new drivers and did he know anybody.

MAY. Are you serious?

ROSA. Serious as a heart attack. This guy and Ty were in the war together and to hear him tell it, they thick as thieves. Ty thinks the guy might even take him on as a partner pretty soon.

MAY. He wouldn't have to be out on the road a lot, would he?

ROSA. *(Amused.)* You really got it bad, girl, you know that? Don't worry, he'd be right here in town. They always start the new guys off local.

MAY. Do you think Tyrone would really put in a good word for him?

ROSA. If I asked him to, but there's something I gotta ask you first and you gotta tell me the truth.

MAY. What is it?

ROSA. Is he really okay?

MAY. Rose, you know I got no reason to lie to you. This morning when we were talking, he seemed like his old self again. He was really Charlie.

ROSA. But how can they be sure?

MAY. I'm sure.

ROSA. Oh, you're sure. The man is home one night and you're sure? *(A beat.)*

MAY. I'm not trying to talk you into anything. You brought it up to me, remember?

ROSA. You're right, you're right! Okay, honey, here's what we'll do. Ty's coming by after work. Did you two kill that bourbon he left here yesterday?

MAY. We didn't touch it.

ROSA. Good. I'll bring him down to meet Charlie, we'll drink up that bourbon with you and see how they get along, then Ty can decide.

MAY. Should I tell Charlie?

ROSA. Of course. Make sure he's on his best behavior.

MAY. How much does Ty know?

ROSA. Not much. I told him Charlie had a bum leg they had to put a pin in. Rehab took longer than they expected it to.

MAY. Nothing else?

ROSA. I figure everybody got a right to tell their own business without no help from me. Besides, Charlie never tries anything on the job, does he?

MAY. No. He always comes home.

ROSA. So! No problem.

MAY. Thanks, Rosa.

ROSA. Don't thank me 'til he gets the job. What time is it?

MAY. Almost eleven.

ROSA. Already? I got a hair appointment at eleven-thirty and if I miss this girl, she won't wait for me. I'll see you later!

MAY. Around three?

ROSA. Make it four. I'll make sure he's in a good mood when we get down here.

MAY. Why don't you just call him?

ROSA. Go to hell! *(Rosa exits as lights go to black.)*

Scene 3

That night. The radio is playing a song like "The Way You Do the Things You Do" by The Temptations.* Charlie enters.

MAY. *(Calling from the bedroom.)* Charlie?

CHARLIE. It's me.

MAY. I'll be right out! *(Charlie is enjoying the music; he snaps his fingers a little, sings a few lines. He notices a small tray with bourbon and four glasses on the counter. He lowers the music and calls to May, still in the bedroom.)*

CHARLIE. We having company? *(May enters from the bedroom. She is wearing the green silk dress she described earlier.)*

MAY. Rosa wants to come down and say welcome home.

CHARLIE. Fine as you look in that dress, she better talk fast.

MAY. *(Teasing; pleased at his response.)* You still like this old dress?

CHARLIE. I used to dream about you in this dress. I used to close my eyes and try to remember how it felt sliding across your skin.

MAY. *(Only half-kidding.)* Maybe I should call and tell them to come another time.

CHARLIE. Them?

MAY. She's got a new man. Tyrone.

CHARLIE. She's always got a new man. You met him?

MAY. He's okay. He left this bourbon for you yesterday.

CHARLIE. For me?

MAY. They came by here on their way to the club. Rosa told him you were coming home.

CHARLIE. What else did she tell him?

MAY. Nothing much. Said you had to go to rehab for your leg.

CHARLIE. Good for her! I don't need no strange Negro looking fish-eyed at me because of some stuff he heard from Rosa. *(Picks up the small bottle.)* At least he got the good stuff. He didn't get much of it, but what he got is top of the line.

MAY. You have any luck today?

CHARLIE. Well, depends on what you mean by luck.

---

* See Special Note on Songs and Recordings on copyright page.

MAY. What happened?

CHARLIE. Must have been two hundred people down there by ten-thirty and they weren't even giving out applications until noon.

MAY. For how many jobs?

CHARLIE. Twenty-five, but I figure, hey! I'm here early. There's only seventeen people in front of me and the ones behind me are of no concern.

MAY. Good for you!

CHARLIE. I haven't got to the good part yet. I stood there for an hour and finally they let in the first group of us. So, I filled out the application, walked over to where they were processing everybody and got in another line until they called me over to sit down in front of this young sister in a power suit and one of those wigs that sits way up on top of your head if you fool enough to wear it, and she looked at my application and she looked at me and then she kind of rolled her eyes and sighed like I was the last thing she wanted to see on a Saturday afternoon.

MAY. What was wrong with it?

CHARLIE. She didn't tell me at first. She asked me about some of the jobs I'd listed and I told her. She asked me about some of the gaps and I told her I'd been in the hospital a couple of times, but I was fine now. She rolled her eyes again when I said that and I assured her that the demands of stacking boxes would probably not be more than I could handle and she said that wasn't the problem. "Well," I said, "what is the goddamn problem?"

MAY. Did you say, "goddamn"?

CHARLIE. Only to myself, of course. To the sister, I just said, "What is the problem?" And you know what she said?

MAY. What?

CHARLIE. She said I was too old. *(He laughs.)*

MAY. Too old?

CHARLIE. Too old to be stacking boxes for a living. They figure I'll be *(As if reciting from memory.)* slow, unreliable and prone to work-related injury.

MAY. That's against the law!

CHARLIE. That's what I told Miss Sweetness and she referred me to her supervisor, who was out to lunch at the time.

MAY. Did you wait for him?

CHARLIE. I started to, but the more I waited, the more I couldn't think of anything I wanted to say when the guy showed up. I couldn't see spending the rest of the afternoon trying to talk somebody into letting me have a job I didn't even want.

MAY. I told you not to go down there in the first place.

CHARLIE. But not because you thought I was too old. Because you thought I was too good, so it's not like you get to say I told you so.

MAY. I never say I told you so.

CHARLIE. You don't think I'm too old, do you, May?

MAY. I think you're in your prime.

CHARLIE. Which is why I love you! When are they coming?

MAY. Any minute now.

CHARLIE. Do I have time to change my shirt?

MAY. Sure. *(Charlie exits to the bedroom. A beat, then May calls to him.)* Charlie?

CHARLIE. Yeah?

MAY. Rosa said they might be hiring on Tyrone's job.

CHARLIE. What job is that?

MAY. He drives a truck.

CHARLIE. *(Comes out buttoning his shirt.)* Yeah? Local or long-distance?

MAY. Local. You know I asked her that first! *(He embraces her.)*

CHARLIE. If I ever do another thing that makes me have to leave your side for longer than eight hours at a time, I want you to do me a favor.

MAY. Anything.

CHARLIE. Shoot me.

MAY. Anything but that. *(The doorbell rings. May starts to answer it, but Charlie stops her.)*

CHARLIE. I got it. *(Charlie opens the door to admit Rosa and Tyrone.)*

ROSA. Charlie Thompson! *(She hugs him warmly.)* Welcome home and meet Tyrone! Ty, this is Charlie.

CHARLIE. Come on in.

TYRONE. Thanks, man. Good to meet you.

CHARLIE. Same here. How's it going, Rose?

ROSA. Same old, same old, but I can't complain.

MAY. Which doesn't mean she won't. Hey, Tyrone.

TYRONE. Hey, May. Looking good, girl! *(Charlie has a visibly negative reaction to Tyrone's playful compliment. No one notices except May, who glances at Charlie nervously.)*

ROSA. Do you have my silver hoops?

MAY. I think so.

ROSA. I need them for this dress, honey. I'm naked without my earrings! We'll be right back. *(Rosa pulls a slightly reluctant May into the bedroom so the men can have a moment alone.)*

TYRONE. *(Looking after May admiringly.)* You a lucky man, brother. *(A beat.)*

CHARLIE. That ain't something you got to tell me.

TYRONE. *(Alerted by Charlie's tone.)* I didn't mean nothing by it.

CHARLIE. I didn't think you did. It just makes a man feel funny when some other muthafucker is as comfortable up in his house as he is. *(Tyrone is not afraid of a possible confrontation, but knows in this case he is guiltless and no confrontation is required. His tone is conciliatory, but direct.)*

TYRONE. It ain't like that, man. You can believe it. Rosa and May too tight for me to be trying to even think something like that. Besides, that woman loves you, man. From what Rose say, she hardly left the house since you been gone. Just sitting around, waitin' on you. This is probably only the third or fourth time I've even seen her at all. *(A beat. Charlie relaxes.)*

CHARLIE. No problem, man. Everything's cool. *(Charlie extends his hand. Tyrone shakes it. Both are grateful that the bad moment has passed.)* I've just been away, that's all. Things can change.

TYRONE. I know what you talkin' about. When I was in 'Nam, brother be gone two weeks and get a letter: "Dear John Henry, love you, but love Jody more. You take care, okay?" Nigga get distracted and get his head blown off, worrying about some woman ten thousand miles away.

CHARLIE. How about a drink?

TYRONE. Don't mind if I do. *(Charlie pours two drinks and hands one to Tyrone.)*

CHARLIE. Here's to good women.

TYRONE. You got that right. *(They touch glasses, drink.)*

CHARLIE. Thanks for the welcome-home taste, brother. Glad you could come by to share it.

TYRONE. No problem, man. I know rehab's a bitch. When I got my arm hurt, I had so much rehab they thought I was on staff at the damn place. Shit works though. You stick with it, it pays off big time.

CHARLIE. What happened to your arm?

TYRONE. I was out on patrol, wadn't nothin' happenin'. Quiet as you please. Sun coming up. Birds singing. I thought maybe the war was over and nobody had told us yet, but soon as you start thinking like that, that's when the shit always happens. Just like clockwork, we got hit hard coming back in. Shrapnel sliced my arm open like a grape. Sucker was hanging on by a thread so this cracker looked at it real fast and told me they were going to have to cut it off. So I picked up my weapon in my good hand and I said, "Doc, if you do, I'll be the last nigga you cut."

CHARLIE. I see he figured out something else to do.

TYRONE. Damn right! If I'd a let that cracker have his way, I'd be wearing a hook for a hand and you know women gonna run from some shit like that.

CHARLIE. I knew a guy with a hook one time. He did all right.

TYRONE. Yeah, but what kind of women we talking about? You paying a woman, she'll tell you she like whatever you got.

CHARLIE. Nice women.

TYRONE. No shit?

CHARLIE. I'll tell you what I learned from that.

TYRONE. What?

CHARLIE. They don't hang around us for our hands. *(A beat, then Tyrone laughs.)*

TYRONE. You a crazy muthafucker, man!

CHARLIE. *(Shares the laugh.)* You got that right.

TYRONE. May said you messed up your leg in Mississippi. What the hell happened? You weren't down there winkin' at them white girls, were you?

CHARLIE. Not me, brother. I was registering people to vote. I ran into a deputy sheriff who didn't appreciate it.

TYRONE. I never did understand that nonviolent shit. No disrespect or anything, but I ain't goin' nowhere if I gotta promise not to kick a cracker's ass if he puts his hands on me. They arrest you?

CHARLIE. Yeah. Broke my leg in three places, threw me in a hole and waited two days before they called somebody to set it.

TYRONE. Damn, man, that's ugly. You might as well have been in 'Nam, but at least when they hit us, we could hit 'em back!

CHARLIE. Sometimes, it seems like it was all one big war, you know? Some over here and some over there, but one thing guaranteed — you weren't coming out the same way you went in.

TYRONE. Mississippi got the meanest crackers God ever made. I know if it's any meaner, I don't wanna see 'em.

CHARLIE. When they threw me in that hole, they looked at me and said, "We're going to be fair about this, nigger. You gonna leave your mind down there or your nuts. You can decide." *(A beat.)* So whenever a muthafucker calls me crazy, I say, goddamn right! *(They laugh and refresh their drinks as Rosa and May enter from the bed-*

33

room. Rosa is now wearing large, silver hoop earrings.)
ROSA. I think they started without us, May. What do you think?
MAY. I think if we hurry we can probably catch up.
TYRONE. It's no rush, ladies. I brought a backup just in case y'all
had already put a hurtin' on this one. *(He produces a larger bottle of
Jack Daniels and refreshes drinks all around.)*
ROSA. Will wonders never cease?
CHARLIE. You finally found you a generous man is all.
TYRONE. Ain't no mystery about that.
ROSA. So can we finally have your official welcome-home toast?
CHARLIE. I think me and the brother have already been there.
ROSA. *(To Tyrone.)* Did you say anything?
TYRONE. Like what?
ROSA. You know, remarks. Suitable for the occasion.
MAY. *(Quickly.)* I'll do it.
ROSA. Thank you. Go ahead, May.
MAY. To Charlie Thompson, man of the people, light of my life,
and all-around good brother. Welcome home, baby. I missed you
like crazy. *(Charlie kisses May.)*
ROSA. Y'all are too sweet!
TYRONE. You miss me like that when I'm hauling distance?
ROSA. I'll get used to it.
TYRONE. If I have anything to do with it, you ain't gettin' used
to a damn thing.
MAY. I used to hate it when Charlie was hauling.
CHARLIE. We spent so much money on telephone bills it wasn't
worth it to make the trip.
TYRONE. You drove a rig?
CHARLIE. Couple of years, off and on. I tried to get them to just
let me work local, but they kept sending me on distance so I quit.
TYRONE. Distance is where the money is.
CHARLIE. *(Looking affectionately at May.)* Money ain't all there is
to think about sometimes.
ROSA. But it never hurts, you know what I'm saying? It never hurts.
TYRONE. That's why I keep this woman close to me, because we
think the same way. She always got one eye on the flow of the cash.
ROSA. And one eye looking out for opportunities.
CHARLIE. Now you sound like an ad for the *Wall Street Journal*.
TYRONE. She's telling the truth. I asked her to do it. In sort of a
semi-official way, right, babe?
ROSA. I prefer quasi-official.

MAY. Do what in a quasi-official way?

ROSA. Look for opportunities.

CHARLIE. What kind of opportunities?

TYRONE. Business, mostly. Right now, I'm concentrating on investigating the trucking business, since that's what I'm doing myself. I figure that's a good place to start.

ROSA. Business is business and I know what it takes to run one without getting taken to the cleaner's. Sonny never could have made that club show a profit without me.

MAY. You're going into business?

TYRONE. Not right away, but some things are opening up for me. I might be able to get in on the ground floor of something good.

ROSA. Tell 'em, honey.

TYRONE. Hey, man, I don't mean to be taking over your party or nothin'.

CHARLIE. Don't you get nervous 'til I get nervous.

TYRONE. Cool. This guy who I'm driving for, we were in 'Nam together. He ain't no whiz kid, but his family is wired in with some people who helped him when he got back. They sold him three trucks cheap and some good routes. Now he's got more business than he can handle. But up to a year ago, I don't know any of this, right? I haven't seen this guy in twenty years. But I'm sitting in a bar one night and this guy walks in and looks at me like he knows me. This ain't a bar I frequent, so I wasn't trying to make no eye contact or nothing, but this guy keeps looking at me. I can see this out of the corner of my eye, but I'm drinking like I'm alone in the room.

ROSA. *(Impatiently.)* Tyrone! The suspense is killing me! Get to the point.

TYRONE. The point is, this is the guy, Neal, that I knew from 'Nam that I haven't seen in all that time, but he recognizes me and now he's telling me how great his business is doing and how much money he's making and how he's gonna buy his brothers out and be his own boss and then he starts getting all sentimental about seeing me 'cause it's like right before Christmas Eve and I saved his life once in the bush, not 'cause I knew it was him, he was just a guy down, screaming, and I grabbed his arm and pulled him in with us before they came back to finish him off and I said, hey, if you feeling so emotional and shit — pardon my French! — if you're feeling so emotional, how about giving me a job? And he was shocked that I could be out of a job, like I was in demand because I'd saved his life, but that was okay because he hired me and once I got in, I could see that there was a lot of improvements he could make. So I told him a couple of things and he tried them and they worked and so I told him a couple more and they worked even better.

CHARLIE. He ought to give you a raise and a desk job.

TYRONE. You reading my mind, man. I just look around at his operation and things jump out at me about how to fix it up first-class. Right now, I'm proving my value to this guy and then I'm going to say, hey, how about taking me in as a partner, let me have a little piece of this pie.

MAY. That sounds real good. Congratulations.

ROSA. Don't be congratulating anybody yet. All that pie is still in the sky so far, but back in the real world, I heard you got my job at Hudson's today.

CHARLIE. It's still open if *you* lookin' for it. They turned me down cold.

ROSA. Turned you down?

CHARLIE. Too old.

TYRONE. Too old for what?

MAY. A warehouse job downtown. Charlie was over there this morning.

TYRONE. You looking for work?

CHARLIE. Yeah.

TYRONE. Why didn't you say so? They're hiring at my place. My buddy asked me if I knew anybody since I been on him about how come I'm the only brother he got working over there. If you want the job, it's yours.

CHARLIE. Just like that?

TYRONE. Hey, man. We all went through the war together, right?

CHARLIE. Thanks a lot, brother. I mean it, but I gotta tell you something. I wasn't kidding about what I said before.

TYRONE. About what?

CHARLIE. About being crazy.

TYRONE. What do you mean?

CHARLIE. They hurt my leg, that's the truth, but that wasn't shit compared to the number they did on my head.

TYRONE. *(Looking at Rosa, who looks away.)* That's why you were in the hospital?

CHARLIE. Yeah.

TYRONE. All summer?

CHARLIE. Yeah.

TYRONE. What kind of crazy are you?

CHARLIE. *(Grinning.)* The nonviolent kind.

TYRONE. So you feeling okay now that you out? You handling it all right?

CHARLIE. What are my other choices? *(A beat, then Tyrone laughs.)*

TYRONE. You got that right! Get your ass a job like the rest of these crazy muthafuckers out here, that's what you better do. *(He takes a scrap of paper from his pocket, writes down the number of the place* Tell him I told you to call. I'll put my name on here, too, and if he offers it, take the job, man. Just don't tell my buddy all that crazy shit. White folks don't need to know everything a nigga know!

CHARLIE. I'll drink to that! *(The men touch glasses to seal the bargain, then drink.)*

ROSA. Well, now that we got that settled, I got a new joke for you, Charlie.

MAY. Oh, Lord!

CHARLIE. You think I'm ready for it, Rosa?

MAY. No! Trust me!

ROSA. Ty thought it was funny.

MAY. Which shows y'all are meant for each other, but it's no reason to torture the rest of us.

ROSA. Come on, Charlie. It's a good one.

CHARLIE. Okay, go ahead.

ROSA. Knock-knock.

CHARLIE. It's a knock-knock joke?

MAY. I warned you.

CHARLIE. *(Laughing.)* Well, if I was ever gonna find it funny, this will be the time. Go ahead, Sister Rosa. Who's there?

ROSA. Banana.

CHARLIE. Banana, who?

ROSA. Knock-knock. *(They continue with the joke as the lights go to black.)*

Scene 4

The following Saturday. Lights up on Rosa and May. May is slowly chewing a piece of pie. In front of her, there are a number of slices of pie on individual saucers. Rosa is holding a clipboard and watching May expectantly. May nods and swallows.

MAY. Mmmmmmmm. It's okay.

ROSA. So on a scale of one to ten, what?

MAY. Ten is the worst?

ROSA. Ten is the best.

MAY. I'd give it a three.

ROSA. You said, "Mmmmmmmm." You can't say, "Mmmmm-mmm," and give it a three.

MAY. I wasn't saying, "Mmmmmmmm," because it tasted so good. I was saying, "Mmmmmmm," because I was thinking.

ROSA. What were you thinking?

MAY. I was thinking it was pretty good, but sort of bland. Needs some cinnamon. And I didn't taste any nutmeg at all.

ROSA. White folks know they can't make no sweet potato pie!

MAY. It wasn't that bad.

ROSA. Then give it a five.

MAY. What difference does it make? You don't get paid more if I like it, do you?

ROSA. I wouldn't be doing this at all if I'd a gone on and taken that 1-900 job like I had some sense.

MAY. I told you Tyrone wouldn't like that.

ROSA. He liked it fine when I did it for him.

MAY. Rosa!

ROSA. I told him the guy said I was a natural and he said he'd like to see for himself. So I told him to go on down to the pay phone and give me a buzz.

MAY. You didn't!

ROSA. I sure did.

MAY. What did he say?

ROSA. That is none of your business, but I will tell you this. He's installing a separate line on Monday so he can call me without standing out in the rain.

MAY. The man said you were a natural.

ROSA. Yeah, but Ty don't want me to make money off it. He sounded like you. Some things are private.

MAY. If I had known telling you that meant I had to eat this much bad sweet potato pie, I would have told you to go for broke.

ROSA. You're lucky. I made Tyrone taste-test the frozen collard greens.

MAY. How were they?

ROSA. How do you think? The beauty of collard greens is the time it takes to make them. If you cut that out, what's the point? Do one more.

MAY. I can't do one more! I'm going to weigh a ton by the time you get your report done.

ROSA. Just think of it this way: You'll be helping to decide which sweet potato pie is on tables all over America.

MAY. I'd rather decide what they watch on TV.

ROSA. They got machines that do that. Sorry. *(They clear away the pie and saucers, put away the clipboard and questionnaires.)*

MAY. Where'd you all go last night?

ROSA. We rented a video. One of those gangster movies. Ty loves 'em, so I'm watching it, but I'm making sure I close my eyes so I don't see the part where they stab the guy in the trunk of the car, I can't take that stuff, and then this one guy is talking to his wife and she's saying how she's worried that he might get caught doing this gangster stuff and what would happen to her if he had to go to jail and he tells her not to worry about it and you know why?

MAY. Why?

ROSA. Because, and these are the actual words he used, "Nobody goes to jail but nigger stick-up men:"

MAY. So?

ROSA. So I didn't appreciate it.

MAY. Didn't appreciate that he said "nigger"?

ROSA. He can say what he wants but I don't have to pay three dollars to hear it.

MAY. You don't think Italian gangsters ever say "nigger"?

ROSA. In real life, I'm sure they do, but it pisses me off in the movies 'cause soon as I hear it, I get mad and miss half the movie 'til I can calm down. I hate that. I was watching this Woody Allen movie one time. It was pretty good, too. All about a bunch of sisters — blood sisters, not soul sisters — sleeping with each other's husbands and driving each other crazy, and right in the middle, when I had already picked one I sort of identified with, here comes the black maid at the party. Sister was dressed in that Hollywood maid outfit — little apron, white orthopedic shoes like a damn nurse in case somebody fell out or something. But it made me mad. She didn't have one line and nobody even said anything directly to her. They took what she was offering on that little silver tray and she glided on by and then back out to the kitchen. That was it. But I couldn't stop thinking about her. Was she pissed off 'cause she had to work? Was she tired? Were they paying her extra to work the holiday since she was there serving their Christmas dinner instead of home serving her own?

MAY. *(Laughing.)* You know what I think?

ROSA. What?

MAY. I think you ought to stop going to the movies.

ROSA. I was home last night. What about that?

MAY. Maybe you should find another form of recreation.

ROSA. When I told Ty to turn it off, he had a few suggestions.

MAY. I'm sure Brother Tyrone is a man of many talents.

ROSA. Many talents and a one-track mind. All Ty's suggestions begin and end with S-E-X.

MAY. What's wrong with S-E-X?

ROSA. Nothing's wrong with it, but rationing is in effect in that area, honey.

MAY. Rationing?

ROSA. Didn't your mama ever tell you nobody buys the cow if they already got the milk?

MAY. My mama told me you catch more flies with honey than you do with vinegar. *(Charlie and Tyrone enter.)* Hey, baby!

ROSA. You two look like the cats who swallowed the canary.

CHARLIE. *(Dramatically.)* The question is, what are you looking at?

ROSA. Don't get me started.

CHARLIE. And the answer is ... tell 'em, Brother Tyrone.

TYRONE. You are looking at a Negro with a job!

CHARLIE. A good job!

MAY. You went down to Neal's today?

CHARLIE. This very day.

MAY. *(Excited and very pleased.)* You didn't even tell me!

TYRONE. They hired him on the spot. I told you, I got pull down there!

CHARLIE. I start Monday. Brother Tyrone will teach me the

route himself, and come Friday, I will bring you home a paycheck!

ROSA. Praise the Lord!

MAY. I knew you'd get it. *(She embraces Charlie happily.)*

TYRONE. Thank you, May. Somebody around here gotta have faith in my connections.

MAY. I got faith in Charlie.

CHARLIE. Eat your heart out, man.

TYRONE. *(Putting an affectionate arm around Rosa.)* I'm not doing bad.

ROSA. Thank you, sweet thing. Want some sweet potato pie?

TYRONE. Is it any good?

MAY. I gave it a three.

ROSA. But she upgraded it to a five!

MAY. How about drinks instead? *(She brings glasses, bourbon and a bowl of ice.)*

CHARLIE. Let's go get something to eat downtown.

ROSA. Listen to Mr. Rockefeller!

TYRONE. Streets are gonna be full of cops.

MAY. Why?

TYRONE. You all didn't hear about it?

ROSA. About what? We haven't been out all day.

TYRONE. They found another body. Throat cut just like the last one.

MAY. White guy?

TYRONE. Yeah. Sixty-five years old. Had money on him, too. Nothing stolen.

MAY. If he keeps going like this, ain't no white folks coming back downtown.

CHARLIE. Why'd you say "he"? What if it's a woman?

ROSA. Those guys were both in their sixties.

CHARLIE. It wouldn't have to be a girlfriend. It could be something political.

TYRONE. Like terrorists?

CHARLIE. Yeah.

MAY. Female terrorists? What country are they from?

CHARLIE. I don't know. I'm just saying, it could be.

MAY. I don't think so. Female terrorists would probably use a gun.

CHARLIE. Too loud.

MAY. But a knife makes you have to get too close. You have to actually touch the person.

CHARLIE. That's true.

41

MAY. Plus, I don't know any women who are mad enough to slit somebody's throat unless it's real personal.

CHARLIE. Slitting somebody's throat is always real personal.

TYRONE. Whoever's doing it, May's right. It's making folks nervous.

ROSA. It's making me nervous!

TYRONE. No, I mean white folks. Nobody mentioned it directly, but all up and down my route, they were much friendlier than usual. Smiling and saying good morning like they wanted to make sure I didn't go off.

MAY. I felt like that after the first one, too. Like the white folks at work were walking on eggs.

CHARLIE. So now we gotta start cutting people's throats to get somebody to say good morning like they got some sense?

ROSA. Let's change the subject. I got a new joke.

MAY. Oh, Lord!

ROSA. Exactly! It's a religious joke.

CHARLIE. It's not a knock-knock joke, is it?

ROSA. My brother told me this one and he's great at telling jokes!

CHARLIE. Can we get him on the phone?

MAY. I'm going to get ice. *(She goes to the kitchen.)*

TYRONE. I'm listening.

ROSA. Thank you, sweet thing. Okay. Jesus and Moses are walking by a lake talking about how bad they both were back in the day and then Jesus says, "What was the baddest thing you ever did?" Moses thought for a second and said, "That Red Sea thing was pretty impressive. How about you?" Jesus didn't even have to think about it. He spoke right up. "Walking on water."

MAY. You didn't say it was a sacrilegious joke.

ROSA. My brother said he heard it from a deacon, so hush! Anyway, Moses agreed that was truly miraculous and since they were right there by the shore and everything he asked Jesus if he could show him a few steps. "I can do better than that," Jesus said. "Let's row out to the middle and I'll walk back with you." So they rowed on out there to the deep water, Moses held the oars and Jesus stepped over the side and sank like a stone. Moses finally pulled him back up in the boat and Jesus was like, "I don't understand. I used to be really good at this." Then Moses said, "I see what the problem is. Last time, you didn't have those holes in your hands and feet." *(They all laugh, relieved and amused.)*

MAY. You are going to hell, girl, sure as I'm sittin' here!

ROSA. I told you I knew how to tell a joke.

CHARLIE. You must have been practicing.

ROSA. You can tell that one to the guys at work and break the ice.

CHARLIE. Not me. If I tell one, they'll tell one and too many of their jokes got me as the punch line.

TYRONE. You got that right. When they get too relaxed, they say something you gotta hit 'em for and they didn't even mean nothin' by it. This guy in 'Nam used to like to hang out with the brothers and a couple of us had to tighten him up one time. After that, if he thought he was out of line, he'd say, "Uh, oh! How close am I to gettin' hit?" *(The men laugh.)*

CHARLIE. You know this guy ain't killed but two people and we're already getting more respect. What if he really goes off and takes out ten or twelve? You'll be a partner by Christmas!

TYRONE. I'll drink to that! *(The men toast.)*

ROSA. That's not funny.

MAY. They're just kidding, Rose.

ROSA. Those are innocent people.

CHARLIE. Sometimes in a war, innocent people die.

ROSA. Does this look like a war to you?

CHARLIE. Do you walk up to the corner at night by yourself?

ROSA. That's not because of any war. That's because of all those young hardheads who don't want to work for a living!

CHARLIE. Ask Brother Tyrone. He'll tell you.

MAY. I thought we were going to change the subject.

CHARLIE. Am I right, Ty?

TYRONE. About what?

CHARLIE. When you blow up a village, innocent people get blown up, too, don't they? *(A beat.)*

TYRONE. Yeah. Sometimes.

CHARLIE. Sometimes innocent people get hurt. That's all I'm saying.

ROSA. You're just talking crazy. *(A beat.)*

CHARLIE. I got a good job, good friends and a good woman. How crazy can I be?

MAY. Well, to have all that, this isn't much of a celebration you're throwing. We need some music!

TYRONE. They're playing old Motown on WJLB all weekend. *(May turns on the radio. It is a song like "Pride and Joy" by Marvin Gaye.*)*

---

* See Special Note on Songs and Recordings on copyright page.

MAY. Come on, Tyrone! Let's show these old-time Negroes what a real bop is! *(May and Tyrone dance.)*
CHARLIE. Come on, Rose. I think we been challenged.
ROSA. By two of the no-dancingest Negroes in Detroit!
TYRONE. That's not what you said at the club last Friday.
ROSA. Times change, sweet thing. Times change! *(They all laugh and dance. The phone rings. May goes to answer it.)*
MAY. Hello? What? Hang on, I can't hear you. *(Charlie turns down the radio. Rosa and Tyrone move away to freshen their drinks.)* Henry? Yeah, what's up? Tomorrow? Can't Caroline go? What about Grace? I know I'm a delegate, Henry, but I'm an alternate, remember? Okay, okay. I hear you. Right. You gonna pick me up? I'm always on time! Yeah, I'll tell him. *(She hangs up the phone.)*
CHARLIE. What's up, babe?
MAY. I gotta go to Chicago tomorrow for the regional union meeting. Caroline broke her ankle and Grace's kids have the mumps. I won't be back until Thursday. Henry says to tell you he's sorry.
CHARLIE. Apologies accepted. *(Watching May.)* So, what's the problem?
MAY. I wanted to be here for your first day down at Neal's.
CHARLIE. So you could pack my lunch and have dinner on the table when I get home?
MAY. Something like that.
CHARLIE. *(Gently.)* We got plenty of time. Things ain't gonna get nothing but better.
MAY. Promise?
CHARLIE. I promise. *(Charlie turns up the music. It is a song like "Forever" by Marvin Gaye.*)* May I have this dance? *(May moves into Charlie's arms and they begin to slow-dance.)*
ROSA. You two are pathetic.
CHARLIE. *(Laughing.)* And I ain't even 'shamed! *(Rosa moves into Tyrone's arms, and they begin to dance.)*
ROSA. Me, neither! *(They all laugh and dance easily as lights fade to black.)*

End of Act One

---

* See Special Note on Songs and Recordings on copyright page.

ACT TWO

Scene 1

The following Friday. Lights up on Charlie alone in the kitchen. He gets a glass from the cabinet, takes an unopened bottle of Jack Daniels from a bag on the coffee table, pours a drink and sits, thinking. The doorbell rings. He ignores it and it rings again, longer. He gets up and opens the door, still holding the drink.

ROSA. Hey, Charlie! I'm on my way for Chinese takeout. Want me to bring you back something?
CHARLIE. I don't think so, but thanks ... *(He does not invite her in, and she glances at him, then notices the drink.)*
ROSA. You're not drinking alone, are you?
CHARLIE. I wouldn't be very good company right now, Rose.
ROSA. You'll do. *(Rosa enters, gets a glass, pours a drink and sits down. Charlie reluctantly closes the door and sits.)*
CHARLIE. Don't say I didn't warn you.
ROSA. I'll keep that in mind. You talk to May?
CHARLIE. Not today.
ROSA. *(Overly casual.)* Why don't you call her? *(A beat.)*
CHARLIE. Relax, Rose. My plans for the evening are very simple. I'm going to lock my door, get real drunk and pass out. That's not against the law yet, is it?
ROSA. If it was, half the Negroes in Detroit would be in the penitentiary. Cheers! *(They toast and drink.)*
CHARLIE. You're eating kind of late, aren't you?
ROSA. You're drinking kind of early, aren't you?
CHARLIE. Then I guess we're even. *(He pours another. A beat.)*
ROSA. What's up, Charlie?
CHARLIE. It's been one of those days, you know?
ROSA. Every day is one of those days, but you ain't been stopping on your way home for a bottle of Jack.

45

CHARLIE. How do you know?

ROSA. May would have told me.

CHARLIE. Why would she do that?

ROSA. Because we're friends. That's what friends do.

CHARLIE. Is it? *(A beat. Rosa will not be distracted.)* I haven't talked to May yet.

ROSA. You already said that.

CHARLIE. I usually talk to her at night.

ROSA. I know. Right before you go to bed.

CHARLIE. May told you that too?

ROSA. She didn't have to. *(A beat.)*

CHARLIE. They gave me a drug test at work.

ROSA. So, how'd you do?

CHARLIE. *(Agitated.)* How'd I do? I failed it, of course! All that shit I take for my head showed up like I was smoking crack or something!

ROSA. Did you tell them you were taking prescription drugs?

CHARLIE. I walked in yesterday morning and BAM. There they were! No talk required.

ROSA. Calm down. Talk to Neal. He'll be able to straighten it out.

CHARLIE. *(Increasingly agitated.)* I tried to talk to him, but he didn't want to hear it. Pretended he hadn't been out drinking a beer with me and Ty last week like we were buddies and shit. All of a sudden he's acting like I came in to stick up the place!

ROSA. Calm down, will you? You didn't start anything down there, did you?

CHARLIE. Start anything? Like what?

ROSA. Like whatever! This job means a lot to Tyrone!

CHARLIE. This job means a lot to me! *(Struggling to regain his composure.)* Listen, Rose. I been to work on time. I do my route. I say good morning and good night. I drive that damn truck all day because that's what I get paid to do, and that's all!

ROSA. Okay, okay! We both need to just calm down. This is not a big crisis. This is a small misunderstanding.

CHARLIE. That's just what I told Neal!

ROSA. Of course you did, but he needs to hear it from Ty.

CHARLIE. *(Sarcastic.)* Somebody he trusts?

ROSA. He trusted him enough to give you a job, didn't he?

CHARLIE. Such as it is.

ROSA. *(Standing to leave.)* You said you weren't fit company tonight. My mistake for not listening.

CHARLIE. Don't go, Rose! I'm sorry. It's just that ... I keep telling May everything is going to be different this time. I don't want to be looking in her face if she ever stops believing me. *(A beat.)* I didn't start anything. I just left.

ROSA. Good. Ty's still on the road, but I'll tell him what happened, he can talk to Neal on the phone and get things straightened around without waiting until he gets back.

CHARLIE. How long before you talk to Ty?

ROSA. About three hours from now. Right before I go to bed. *(A beat. They both relax a little.)* You not the only one with some romance in your life, you know?

CHARLIE. You really think Ty can talk to Neal? Tell him this kind of response is not required?

ROSA. I keep trying to tell you and your hardheaded wife that's what friends are for!

CHARLIE. Do me a favor and don't mention this to May. I don't want to worry her.

ROSA. Tell her once it's all squared away. Show her you knew how to handle it.

CHARLIE. Thanks, Rose. *(A beat.)*

ROSA. You and May got something good, Charlie. Hold onto it.

CHARLIE. I don't deserve that woman.

ROSA. Yes, you do. Can't nobody else put up with either one of your high-strung asses.

CHARLIE. You're doing all right.

ROSA. Don't push your luck! *(She prepares to go.)* So, you're not up for Chinese, how about some Cuban food?

CHARLIE. My treat.

ROSA. What's the occasion?

CHARLIE. No occasion. That's what friends do. *(They exit as lights go to black.)*

Scene 2

Monday. Lights up on May vacuuming the room. A dust cloth and other light cleaning supplies are in evidence. Rosa rings the doorbell several times before May hears it and opens the door. Rosa is carrying a homemade sweet potato pie with foil over the top.

ROSA. Welcome back.

MAY. What's this?

ROSA. A real sweet potato pie. Made it myself. I figure you earned it.

MAY. Come on in. I'm just cleaning things. You know if you leave a man alone in a house for a week, it's a miracle it's still standing when you get back.

ROSA. Charlie home?

MAY. He's at work.

ROSA. At work? *(May takes the pie to the kitchen; she doesn't notice Rosa's surprised expression.)*

MAY. He said he's been doing double shifts the whole time I was gone. What's wrong?

ROSA. Nothing. How was Chicago?

MAY. Who knows? I didn't hardly get out of the hotel. Those Negroes went there to argue, not to sightsee.

ROSA. You talk to my brother?

MAY. I did. He said call him. He's got another joke for you.

ROSA. I sure need one.

MAY. What's wrong?

ROSA. I don't know. Just seems like the world is going crazy.

MAY. I told you that a long time ago.

ROSA. You hear what happened on Belle Isle last weekend?

MAY. What?

ROSA. A bunch of people were over there, you know how they do on Sunday, drinking and smoking weed, playing music, cooking out. Same old, same old, blase, blase. So the day is over, time to go home and Miss Girl climbs in her car with her friends. They're driving home, talking and laughing, and she gets distracted, probably talking about some man with her girlfriends and she taps the bumper of this guy's car in front of her and he goes berserk. Jumps out, hollering and threatening to kill her, so she freaks, tries to pull around him and get away, but she taps his damn car again, still nothing major, but the guy takes this as a personal affront to his manhood, such as it is, reaches in the car, drags her out, beats her like a dog right there on the bridge and then tells his buddies to hold her while he goes to his car to get a tire iron so he can beat her some more.

MAY. My God! Where were the cops?

ROSA. Who knows? It gets worse. Of course the girl is really freaking by now, not to mention already beat up pretty bad, and her girlfriends are screaming and begging these guys to stop, but they just laugh, and the other people on the bridge are blowing their horns or getting out to look, but ain't none of them getting near homeboy with the tire iron, so Miss Girl looks around for the help she suddenly realizes ain't there and ain't expected and she's so scared she jumps off the bridge. Can't even swim and she jumps off the Belle Isle Bridge into the river. You know what kinda fall that is? Plus, she's still so scared, when two brothers jump in to try and help, she won't let them get anywhere near her. Finally, she goes down and doesn't come up again. They didn't even find her body for two days. *(A beat.)* Now how can somebody get that mad about a scratch on a damn car?

MAY. You know that wasn't about a car.

ROSA. Well, what was it about then? *(A beat.)*

MAY. I don't know.

ROSA. May?

MAY. Yeah?

ROSA. I gotta ask you something, and it may sound funny, but I'm serious, okay?

MAY. Okay. *(A beat.)*

ROSA. Where is Charlie working?

MAY. Down at Neal's with Tyrone, of course, where do you think?

ROSA. No, May.

MAY. No, what?

ROSA. Maybe I should let Charlie tell you.

MAY. Tell me what?

ROSA. He made me promise, otherwise you know I would have called you.

MAY. Either you tell me what you're talking about or I'm calling

Neal's right now.

ROSA. Charlie doesn't work there anymore.

MAY. What do you mean?

ROSA. He got fired.

MAY. Fired for what?

ROSA. He failed a drug test.

MAY. He isn't doing any drugs!

ROSA. He said they were prescription.

MAY. You know they are! He can get a letter from his doctor. Didn't he tell Tyrone?

ROSA. Ty's been on the road, but he called Neal after he talked to Charlie.

MAY. And?

ROSA. May, I don't want to be in the middle of anything. I just stuck my head in to see if he wanted any Chinese takeout since you were gone and eveything and —

MAY. Rosa … *(A beat.)*

ROSA. Tyrone said when he told Neal it was because Charlie was — because of a mental condition — Neal said if he was that crazy, he was too crazy to be driving a truck.

MAY. Did he say that to Charlie?

ROSA. No. Ty had to tell him.

MAY. He didn't say anything to me about it.

ROSA. Ty said Neal was really pissed off at him for even bringing Charlie around.

MAY. We talked on the phone every day. He picked me up last night. He never said a word.

ROSA. I'm sorry, honey. This isn't the way for you to hear it, but when you said he was work —

MAY. It's okay, Rose.

ROSA. Ty's coming off the road in another couple of days. Once everything is straightened out, maybe we can all get together.

MAY. He never said a word.

ROSA. I know. *(A beat.)* I'm gonna go on then. *(She goes to the door.)*

MAY. Rosa? Thanks.

ROSA. Call me.

MAY. I will. *(Rosa exits. May puts away the vacuum and the dusting cloth. Charlie enters.)*

CHARLIE. Hey, May.

MAY. Hey, Charlie.

CHARLIE. You okay?

MAY. Rosa told me what happened.

CHARLIE. What happened about what?

MAY. She said you got fired.

CHARLIE. I can explain about that.

MAY. Why didn't you tell me?

CHARLIE. Because I knew I could fix it.

MAY. You should have told me!

CHARLIE. But I fixed it.

MAY. How did you fix it?

CHARLIE. I called the hospital from Neal's office and they told him the medication was legal and I was okay to drive any truck he had keys for. After that, he said he was sorry he hadn't listened to me before and if I wanted my job back, I could have it.

MAY. That's not what Tyrone said.

CHARLIE. Ty's been on the road all week. I didn't talk to Neal until this morning.

MAY. Are you sure that's what he said? *(Charlie goes to the phone.)*

CHARLIE. You can ask him yourself if you want to.

MAY. No. I just wish that you had told me.

CHARLIE. I didn't want to worry you. Besides, I'm telling you now. *(She moves away from him to the window. She wants to believe him, but she is still unconvinced. She speaks without taking her eyes off the bridge, almost to herself.)*

MAY. When we first moved in, the thing I really liked about this place was that I could wake up every day and be someplace that wasn't here. I could just walk across that bridge and everything was different. The money, the street names, the politics. Everything. There was a whole country where not a living soul knew my name. *(Turns to him.)* You know, if you ever lie to me, it changes everything.

CHARLIE. I know. *(He holds out a small brown paper bag to her.)* These are for you.

MAY. What is it? *(He dumps out the contents. There are ten small packets of seeds for assorted flowers and vegetables.)* Seeds?

CHARLIE. How long you been talking about moving to Canada and planting a garden?

MAY. A long time.

CHARLIE. I just might be ready to take you up on it.

MAY. When?

CHARLIE. I only want to work for Neal for a year. He feels so bad about what happened, he'll give me all the hours I want. If we can save most of that money, we'll have a stake. We can buy a little piece of land off in the woods, where I don't have to see anybody but you. We'll plant flowers in the front and food in the back. And when it starts snowing, we'll put some logs on the fireplace and we won't come out until it's spring.

MAY. I know that dream. I used to stand here when you were gone sometimes and dream it over and over like a movie. I read books about what would grow over there and what wouldn't. I knew what phase of the moon was the best one to plant squash and pumpkins. I had a whole catalogue with nothing but tomatoes in it. I used to stand right here and say their names like the multiplication tables. Red Plum. Green Zebra. Big Rainbow. Yellow Pear. Ultra Pink. Sun Gold. Super Sweet 100. *(A beat.)* I want us to get old together in peace. What do you want?

CHARLIE. That's all I ever wanted.

MAY. No, it isn't. You wanted to change the world, remember?

CHARLIE. I did a hell of a job.

MAY. You could have done worse.

CHARLIE. I could have done a lot better by you.

MAY. Okay. So in this life you owe me. In the next one, I'll make you pay through the nose.

CHARLIE. I'll never lie to you, May.

MAY. *(Teasing him.)* You better not. Nonviolence was only a phase I was going through. *(The bridge illuminates, and they silently share the beauty of the lights.)*

CHARLIE. They're coming, May. You know that?

MAY. What's coming, Charlie?

CHARLIE. Better days.

MAY. You promise?

CHARLIE. I promise. Now tell me what else you're going to grow in my garden.

MAY. Your garden?

CHARLIE. Our garden?

MAY. I like the sound of that.

CHARLIE. Me, too. *(He puts his arms around her gently as the lights go to black.)*

Scene 3

The next day, afternoon. Lights up on May and Rosa. May is rubbing lotion into her hands. There are several small, numbered bottles of lotion in front of her. Rosa, again with a clipboard, is sitting expectantly in front of May.

MAY. This one feels pretty good.
ROSA. One to ten.
MAY. Nine.
ROSA. How about the smell?
MAY. Seven.
ROSA. How can you give the feel a nine and the smell a seven?
MAY. It feels better than it smells.
ROSA. Okay. Would you buy it?
MAY. No.
ROSA. Why not?
MAY. I don't like the smell.
ROSA. You gave it a seven.
MAY. It wasn't disgusting. I just don't like it.
ROSA. This is getting on my nerves. Enough! Wipe it off!
MAY. *(Picks up another one.)* I kind of liked this one.
ROSA. It's on the house.
MAY. Thanks.
ROSA. I'm real glad everything worked out with Neal and Charlie.
MAY. Me, too. I wish he had told me, but I'm just glad it's over.
ROSA. Tyrone will be back tonight. Want to get together later?
MAY. Are you sure you want company? Ty's been gone almost a week.
ROSA. Don't worry. We won't stay long.
MAY. This job is the best thing that's happened to Charlie in a long time. It's like one good thing brings another and another.
ROSA. The opposite is true, too. Bad luck can multiply quicker than any winning streak I ever saw.
MAY. You're a pessimist.
ROSA. I'm a realist. *(A knock. May opens the door to Tyrone, who walks in quickly without being asked.)*
TYRONE. Hey, May. Charlie here? *(He is very agitated.)*

MAY. No, but somebody you know is.

ROSA. *(Moves to embrace him.)* When'd you get back, sweet thing?

TYRONE. *(Moves away from her before she makes contact.)* Six hours ago.

ROSA. *(Surprised.)* Six hours? Why didn't you call me?

TYRONE. I've been talking to the police.

MAY. The police?

TYRONE. I was in Neal's office trying to be sure he wasn't holding nothing about Charlie against me and two cops came and knocked on the door. They found another body downtown this morning and there was a piece of paper lying there right next to the guy with Neal's number and my name on it! My name! Three dead crackers and the cops got my name!

ROSA. My God, Ty! What did they say?

TYRONE. They asked me a lot of questions. Where was I last night? Did I know the guy? One of them asked me if I was in 'Nam. I said yeah, I was in 'Nam, so what? And he said, the way these guys got it, looked like some Green Beret shit or something. It was clean like the guy knew what he was doing. I said that ain't me, man. We didn't do no knife stuff. We had guns, man. Guns! Only those crazy muthafuckers who like to go behind the lines and shit, that's who was cutting people's throats! Not me!

ROSA. They don't think you had anything to do with it, do they?

TYRONE. What do you think I'm talking about? I'm a suspect! They told me not to go anywhere. What do you think that means?

ROSA. But you can't help it if somebody wrote your name on a piece of paper!

TYRONE. *(Rising agitation.)* But who, Rose? Who wrote my name on a piece of paper?

ROSA. How should I know? When the cops figure it out, they'll talk to him and not you. It's all just a mistake!

TYRONE. I wrote it! It's my handwriting. My fingerprints because it's the paper I wrote on sitting right here when I told Charlie about the job! When I opened my goddamn mouth and invited him to fuck up my life!

MAY. You think Charlie ... *(Tyrone just looks at May.)* That's crazy!

TYRONE. No, he's crazy! But it's not going down like this. Not like this here!

ROSA. Just calm down, both of you! We can figure this out. You have alibis. You're innocent!

TYRONE. Listen, Rose. The cops want to arrest somebody. They don't care if it's the nigger who did it or not. They just need to say they got him. And now they got my name on the paper! No — they got me!

ROSA. *(Rising panic as she realizes how serious this really is.)* Charlie can tell them, Ty. When he comes home, he can just tell them!

TYRONE. Tell them what?

ROSA. That you gave that paper to him so he could call Neal about a job.

TYRONE. Is he gonna tell them how it got down there layin' on the ground beside a dead man?

MAY. Stop it!

TYRONE. Where is he?

MAY. He's at work.

TYRONE. At work where?

MAY. He's doing his regular route.

TYRONE. Neal fired him last week!

MAY. Charlie called the hospital! The doctor told Neal —

TYRONE. Neal told me if he saw Charlie anywhere around he was gonna call the police. But I guess he didn't have to. They came on their own! To talk to me! Because of that crazy muthafucker, I'm in the middle of all of it. *(A beat.)* If you see him, tell him I'm looking for him. *(He starts to exit.)*

ROSA. Ty! Wait!

TYRONE. Leave me alone, Rosa. Can't you just leave me alone? *(He exits. A beat.)*

ROSA. Where do you think he is?

MAY. I don't know.

ROSA. How could that paper have gotten there?

MAY. I don't know.

ROSA. Well, he'll come home, won't he?

MAY. I don't know! I don't know! *(A beat.)*

ROSA. I have to ask you, May.

MAY. *(A warning.)* Don't.

ROSA. Do you think he could have done it?

MAY. No.

ROSA. I don't believe you.

MAY. Then get out of my house.

ROSA. No! I won't. Tyrone is a suspect! They think it's him!

MAY. They don't know who it is.

ROSA. This isn't a game, May.

MAY. He's sick!

ROSA. He's killing people!

MAY. It's not true.

ROSA. He's killing innocent people!

MAY. He is an innocent person!

ROSA. Not anymore! Don't you see? Not anymore! *(She goes to the door.)*

MAY. Rose! *(Rosa stops.)* You're my best friend. I need you to be my best friend.

ROSA. *(Gently, but determined.)* We've got to call the police, honey. There's no way around it.

MAY. He can't go to jail. Don't you understand? He's been to jail.

ROSA. And that was wrong, but this is wrong, too.

MAY. You don't understand.

ROSA. Make me! Make me understand!

MAY. We were so young, Rose. We were babies. *(A beat.)* We had been out all day trying to get people to come down to the courthouse to register and we didn't get a single one. All day long, trudging up to these little houses, hoping somebody was home. Some of them were so scared when they realized who we were and what we were talking about that they ran in the house and slammed the door. So we were tired and discouraged and we had a long walk back to the Hemphills and it was already getting dark. I knew we needed to hurry, but I wanted to sit down for a minute and catch my breath.

So we walked a little ways off the road and sat down and Charlie put his arm around me but I was so tired and scared and evil, I just sat there. So he started talking about how important it was for us to be in Mississippi and how much he loved me and how he was going to tell our children how brave their mama was and I sort of leaned on him a little bit and he started kissing me and we just forgot everything. Just for a minute. I know it wasn't more than a minute ...

And then they were shining their flashlights in our faces. They took us to the jail, the sheriff and two deputies, and they locked the front door, and they locked the back door, and they took us down in the basement. At first I thought they were just trying to scare us. They had made a white girl play Russian roulette a couple of days ago until she broke down and started begging them to just let her go home. So I kept demanding the right to call our lawyer until they got mad and told me to shut up and I did.

Then they told Charlie they had a choice for him. They told him he could beat me for having such a smart mouth or he could watch while they finished what he had started by the side of the road. Charlie kept trying to talk to them, telling them if they just let us go, we wouldn't press charges. They laughed at that. Asked him if he'd seen any FBI agents around lately and telling him to choose, but he wouldn't.

Finally, they said, "Okay. This nigger must want us to show him how it's done," and one of the deputies told me to take my clothes off. Then Charlie said, "Stop! Don't touch her. I'll do it." I begged him not to. I didn't care what they did to me, but I was in love with sweet Charles. He was the only man I'd ever had ... The other deputy took off his belt and gave it to Charlie and I know what he meant to do was just pretend and not really hurt me. I know that! But they knew that too, and they wouldn't let him.

They stood right there and made him hit me harder and harder. I started screaming so they'd let him stop, but they wouldn't. They just laughed and said, "Go on, nigger. We'll tell you when to quit." So they made him beat me half to death and then that one who had told me to take my clothes off pulled my dress over my face and did it anyway. They all did it anyway. Right in front of Charlie.

But see, I knew that already. That's what I kept trying to tell him. I don't care what they do to me, but not you. I can't take it from you.

I had to go home after that. My father came to get me. I was hurt so bad, I couldn't have stayed if I wanted to, which I didn't. My mother, my aunts, my father, all of them went crazy. I thought they would tell me how sorry they were. I thought they would hold my hand and put a cold towel on my head or something, but that wasn't it. That wasn't what they wanted at all. They wanted to fuss. They came to tell me how dumb I was for going in the first place. How next time maybe I'd listen to them and keep my behind at home where it belonged. They were afraid to even look at me. I was living proof of something so terrible nobody wanted to think about it, so they got mad at me instead.

My grandmother was the only one who didn't say anything. She'd just come and sit there by me in the dark. I'd wake up and I could hear her crying. Maybe she could hear me crying, too.

My father was so mad, he couldn't talk to me at all. My mother told me it was killing him to know that somebody had beat his baby worse than you would beat a dog and there was nothing he could do about it. I kept trying to tell her yes there was. What he could do was come and hold me. What he could do was tell me how much he loved me and promise that nobody was ever going to hurt me like that again.

I decided I wasn't going back to school in the fall. I didn't see the point. Not just in school, but the point of anything. I kept trying to get my mind around what had happened, but I couldn't. It didn't make any sense to me. What they had done, what they were still doing. It was like it had all happened on another planet. Charlie used to call me a lot. I know it was hard for him to get to a phone, but he did it. My mother was afraid he'd talk me into going back so she'd tell him I was asleep, but I'd hear the phone ring and grab it before she could hang up. Neither one of us knew what to say. He'd ask me how I was doing and I'd say better and then I'd ask him how he was doing and he'd lie and tell me he was okay. After that, we'd just sort of hold the phone until one of us started crying and then we'd hang up.

Then one night, one of the other volunteers called to tell me that Charlie had been arrested again, by the same ones who had picked us up before, and this time, they had taken him to Parchman Prison. I just prayed for him. I didn't know what else to do. Two weeks later she called to tell me they had gotten him out, but his leg was broken in three places and he was in the hospital in Jackson. They held him at Parchman for two weeks and did everything they could think of to him, and never even charged him with anything. I left for Mississippi that night.

When I got to the hospital, I walked in and he reached for me like he was drowning so I took his hand and told him I would never let it go. *(A beat.)* I thought we would die in that room, but we didn't. When Charlie was well enough, we came here but his family didn't know what to do with him anymore than mine knew what to do with me, so we got married and found this place and we just holed up and tried to make sense of it. He used to say we were like desperadoes, drinking bourbon at the border and planning our getaways ... But we couldn't figure out a way to talk about what had happened to us in Mississippi and we couldn't find a way to talk around it. We just sort of hoped it would go away, but it didn't. It got bigger and scarier and bigger and scarier until Charlie couldn't touch me anymore without crying.

ROSA. Oh, May ...

MAY. When we first got back, people broke down. Went crazy. Started doing all kinds of drugs. So many of us were destroyed, Rose. We don't even realize it until something really awful happens and then we say, "Oh, my God! We're not that messed up, are we?" There wasn't anybody to tell. Not just what happened. How it felt. People like to say how brave you are, but they don't want to hear about how scared you were. How you screamed so long you lost your voice and tried to close your mind so you could be someplace else, anyplace else, but there. But what if they don't kill you? What if all the stuff on you heals up except your heart and you can't believe it really happened because if it ever really happened, wouldn't it change the world forever?

ROSA. It did change the world forever.

MAY. Did it? *(A beat.)*

ROSA. You always talk about what happened to Charlie. What about what happened to you, May?

MAY. I survived it. He didn't.

ROSA. That doesn't make it right.

MAY. Nothing makes it right.

ROSA. I'm sorry.

MAY. *(Suddenly angry.)* You're sorry? Sorry for what? Sorry Charlie's so messed up? Sorry they hurt me so bad I could never have his babies? Sorry they took our whole lives from us in one mean Mississippi summer? *(Purposely cruel.)* Or are you just sorry Tyrone probably won't get to be a partner so you can tell him how to do business without getting taken to the cleaner's?

ROSA. That's not fair!

MAY. Where were you when it was time to change the world, Rose? Where the fuck were you? *(Rosa, suddenly frightened of May's rage, exits. May sits down and buries her face in her hands as the lights go to black.)*

Scene 4

That night. The apartment is dark. The bridge is illuminated outside and provides enough light for us to see Charlie sitting alone. May enters, not realizing he is there, and reaches to turn on the light.

CHARLIE. Don't turn on the light, May.

MAY. Charlie! Where were you? I've been all over — !

59

CHARLIE. Do you remember that story?

MAY. What story?

CHARLIE. The story about the Africans. Don't you remember it?

MAY. Which Africans?

CHARLIE. West Coast Africans. Igbos, I think. From Nigeria.

MAY. Can I turn on the light?

CHARLIE. *(Insistent.)* I want you to remember the story.

MAY. And then can I turn on the light?

CHARLIE. Yes.

MAY. Tell me about the Africans.

CHARLIE. They were trying to make them slaves, remember? Rounded 'em up, loaded 'em in, and started back across the ocean with 'em, but when they got here and let 'em out so the people who were going to buy 'em could count their teeth, and figure out which one to mate with which other one, all those Africans just turned around and walked right back into the water. All of 'em. Men, women, children, the whole shipload full of 'em, just walked those chains right on into the ocean. White folks couldn't do nothin' but watch their money wash away to sea. And they all drowned, May. Every single one of 'em. Dead. But they didn't even care, and you know why?

MAY. Why, Charlie?

CHARLIE. Because they believed their spirits would travel home to their ancestors as long as their heads were not separated from their bodies. As long as the head and the heart stayed together, they didn't give a damn about dying. *(May turns on the light. Charlie is wearing a sleeveless undershirt.)*

MAY. Where's your shirt?

CHARLIE. I threw it away.

MAY. Why?

CHARLIE. There was blood on it.

MAY. Blood? What happened? *(Throughout this scene, there is about Charlie a strange and growing peace. He is not happy, but he is finally unafraid.)*

CHARLIE. They won, May. I thought I had figured it out. I thought I could even things up a little. Reclaim what they took from me down in that hole, but I can't, because I was wrong about what they took. I thought they took my mind, but I was still thinking. Then I thought they took my heart, but I was still feeling. Then I thought they took my soul, but I still had you, May, and I thought that could be enough. I thought that could be everything, but I didn't think about one thing. I didn't consider the one thing I thought nobody could take, just because, but I was wrong. I was wrong. There's nothing they can't take if they want it. So they took it, May. They took the part that can feel something besides anger all the damn time. The part that knows how to touch a woman like she's too delicate to bear the weight of your hands. Can you believe it, May? They took my head and separated it from my heart, from my memories. They have drugs designed especially to do that. To make sure what you know doesn't fuck with you to the point where you might actually have to do something about it. And you're right, May. Once you start lying, it changes everything because once you start, you can't stop. And after a while, you don't even want to.

MAY. Charlie, for God's sake, what happened?

CHARLIE. You remember when I told you about the letter? About the doctor writing to his woman while he should have been writing about me? That was the first lie. That was my letter to you, May. A letter I wrote on my skin every day. Forgive me, baby. I'm so sorry.

MAY. Sorry for what? What did you do?

CHARLIE. You know those guys they've been finding downtown?

MAY. Yes.

CHARLIE. That was the second lie.

MAY. You're not making any sense!

CHARLIE. I killed them. I killed all three of them.

MAY. Charlie, why?

CHARLIE. All those years, I thought it was fear that was driving me crazy. I thought that big gray fog inside my head was a great big ball of being scared. Scared of the power they had to treat me like an animal or make me act like one. Scared that if they asked me now, today, I still wouldn't know enough to look that cracker in the eye and say, "I don't care what you do to me, I'm not going to raise my hand to this woman!" But it wasn't fear I was running from, May. That's what the drugs make you think and the therapy and the doctors — all bullshit! It wasn't fear I was running from. It was the anger, May, because I couldn't protect you. I couldn't forget and you couldn't forgive me for remembering.

MAY. I never blamed you for anything. There was nothing you could do.

CHARLIE. I could have made them kill me.

MAY. But I didn't die.

CHARLIE. I ran for thirty years, May, and then I let it catch me and I picked out three, just like those three in Mississippi picked

61

us out, and I did what a man is supposed to do. And I'm sorry, May. Not for the killing. For all those years I didn't kill anybody. I wasted thirty years. My father wasted seventy. My uncles made eighty and never killed a soul, so I owe, May. I owe for all those other crazy Negroes who didn't understand that all we have to do to get sane is —

MAY. No, Charlie! No. We don't have to do it that way.

CHARLIE. Yeah, May, we do. Because that's the only thing they understand. Not love. Not peace. Not God. Not family. All they know is blood. *(A beat.)* And you know the worst part? All that killing? It didn't change a damn thing except me.

MAY. We have to go away, Charlie. They're going to come looking for you here.

CHARLIE. *(He leans back, closes his eyes.)* I'm tired, May. I'm just so tired.

MAY. We'll go to Canada. Tonight. You and me. We'll go so deep in the woods they'll never find us and we'll figure it out, Charlie. We'll figure it all out.

CHARLIE. To Canada?

MAY. Just like we talked about.

CHARLIE. Why did we wait so long?

MAY. So you could get well, Charlie. We had to wait until you got well.

CHARLIE. Tell me about the garden.

MAY. *(Getting up quickly.)* I need to put some things in a bag for us, Charlie. It's time to go! *(Charlie catches May's hand as she starts toward the bedroom.)*

CHARLIE. Better days, May? That's the third lie.

MAY. *(Pleading.)* Please, Charlie. *(Charlie pulls May back down beside him gently but firmly.)*

CHARLIE. Just tell me about the garden. *(A beat. May stops resisting him and tries to calm down.)*

MAY. There's flowers in the front and vegetables in the back. There's carrots and collard greens and corn and sweet potatoes.

CHARLIE. Is there enough sun? *(May enters fully into his fantasy, cuddling closer.)*

MAY. There's good sun all over. And in the wintertime, we'll have a sleigh and we'll go for rides in the snow and put bells on the horses and chestnuts on the fire like in that song you like. And we'll build a little house like the Hemphills had where you can stand in the front and see clear through to the back and there's nothing inside but love.

Just me and you and a whole lot of love.

CHARLIE. Tell me about the tomatoes.

MAY. We grow the best for miles. They're so big and red and juicy that when you eat them the juice runs down your chin and — *(There is a sudden and very loud knocking on the door. This is clearly the police, and the knocking is very loud, intimidating and urgent. May freezes.)*

CHARLIE. *(As if he hears nothing.)* What kind do we grow, May? *(A beat. She tries to put the knocking out of her mind, focusing fully on Charlie's face.)*

MAY. We grow all kinds. *(More knocking, even louder, more insistent. It sounds like it will break down the door, and it continues as May recites the names of the tomatoes and the lights fade to black.)* We grow Red Plum. Green Zebra. Big Rainbow. Yellow Pear. Ultra Pink. Sun Gold. Super Sweet 100 ... *(In the darkness, the insistent knocking continues for several seconds and then stops abruptly.)*

End of Play

PROPERTY LIST

Magazines (MAY)
Envelope with photos and newspaper clipping (MAY)
Makeup (ROSA)
Sandwich (MAY)
Pint bottle and larger bottle of Jack Daniels (TYRONE)
Four glasses (ROSA)
Cup of coffee (CHARLIE, MAY)
Tray of bourbon, glasses (MAY)
Paper, pen (TYRONE)
Pie slices on saucers (MAY)
Clipboard, pen (ROSA)
Glasses, bourbon, ice (MAY)
Glass, bottle of Jack Daniels (CHARLIE)
Glass (ROSA)
Vacuum, cleaning supplies (MAY)
Pie with foil (ROSA)
Brown paper bag with seed packets (CHARLIE)
Small bottles of lotion (MAY)

SOUND EFFECTS

Doorbell
Phone ring

NEW PLAYS

★ **THE EXONERATED by Jessica Blank and Erik Jensen.** Six interwoven stories paint a picture of an American criminal justice system gone horribly wrong and six brave souls who persevered to survive it. "The #1 play of the year...intense and deeply affecting..." *–NY Times.* "Riveting. Simple, honest storytelling that demands reflection." *–A.P.* "Artful and moving...pays tribute to the resilience of human hearts and minds." *–Variety.* "Stark...riveting...cunningly orchestrated." *–The New Yorker.* "Hard-hitting, powerful, and socially relevant." *–Hollywood Reporter.* [7M, 3W] ISBN: 0-8222-1946-8

★ **STRING FEVER by Jacquelyn Reingold.** Lily juggles the big issues: turning forty, artificial insemination and the elusive scientific Theory of Everything in this Off-Broadway comedy hit. "Applies the elusive rules of string theory to the conundrums of one woman's love life. Think *Sex and the City* meets *Copenhagen*." *–NY Times.* "A funny offbeat and touching look at relationships...an appealing romantic comedy populated by oddball characters." *–NY Daily News.* "Where kooky, zany, and madcap meet...whimsically winsome." *–NY Magazine.* "STRING FEVER will have audience members happily stringing along." *–TheaterMania.com.* "Reingold's language is surprising, inventive, and unique." *–nytheatre.com.* "...[a] whimsical comic voice." *–Time Out.* [3M, 3W (doubling)] ISBN: 0-8222-1952-2

★ **DEBBIE DOES DALLAS adapted by Erica Schmidt, composed by Andrew Sherman, conceived by Susan L. Schwartz.** A modern morality tale told as a comic musical of tragic proportions as the classic film is brought to the stage. "A scream! A saucy, tongue-in-cheek romp." *–The New Yorker.* "Hilarious! DEBBIE manages to have it all: beauty, brains and a great sense of humor!" *–Time Out.* "Shamelessly silly, shrewdly self-aware and proud of being naughty. Great fun!" *–NY Times.* "Racy and raucous, a lighthearted, fast-paced thoroughly engaging and hilarious send-up." *–NY Daily News.* [3M, 5W] ISBN: 0-8222-1955-7

★ **THE MYSTERY PLAYS by Roberto Aguirre-Sacasa.** Two interrelated one acts, loosely based on the tradition of the medieval mystery plays. "... stylish, spine-tingling...Mr. Aguirre-Sacasa uses standard tricks of horror stories, borrowing liberally from masters like Kafka, Lovecraft, Hitchcock...But his mastery of the genre is his own...irresistible." *–NY Times.* "Undaunted by the special-effects limitations of theatre, playwright and *Marvel* comic-book writer Roberto Aguirre-Sacasa maps out some creepy twilight zones in THE MYSTERY PLAYS, an engaging, related pair of one acts...The theatre may rarely deliver shocks equivalent to, say, *Dawn of the Dead*, but Aguirre-Sacasa's work is fine compensation." *–Time Out.* [4M, 2W] ISBN: 0-8222-2038-5

★ **THE JOURNALS OF MIHAIL SEBASTIAN by David Auburn.** This epic one-man play spans eight tumultuous years and opens a uniquely personal window on the Romanian Holocaust and the Second World War. "Powerful." *–NY Times.* "[THE JOURNALS OF MIHAIL SEBASTIAN] allows us to glimpse the idiosyncratic effects of that awful history on one intelligent, pragmatic, recognizably real man..." *–NY Newsday.* [3M, 5W] ISBN: 0-8222-2006-7

★ **LIVING OUT by Lisa Loomer.** The story of the complicated relationship between a Salvadoran nanny and the Anglo lawyer she works for. "A stellar new play. Searingly funny." *–The New Yorker.* "Both generous and merciless, equally enjoyable and disturbing." *–NY Newsday.* "A bitingly funny new comedy. The plight of working mothers is explored from two pointedly contrasting perspectives in this sympathetic, sensitive new play." *–Variety.* [2M, 6W] ISBN: 0-8222-1994-8

DRAMATISTS PLAY SERVICE, INC.
440 Park Avenue South, New York, NY 10016 212-683-8960 Fax 212-213-1539
postmaster@dramatists.com www.dramatists.com

NEW PLAYS

★ **MATCH by Stephen Belber.** Mike and Lisa Davis interview a dancer and choreographer about his life, but it is soon evident that their agenda will either ruin or inspire them—and definitely change their lives forever. "Prolific laughs and ear-to-ear smiles." *–NY Magazine.* "Uproariously funny, deeply moving, enthralling theater. Stephen Belber's MATCH has great beauty and tenderness, and abounds in wit." *–NY Daily News.* "Three and a half out of four stars." *–USA Today.* "A theatrical steeplechase that leads straight from outrageous bitchery to unadorned, heartfelt emotion." *–Wall Street Journal.* [2M, 1W] ISBN: 0-8222-2020-2

★ **HANK WILLIAMS: LOST HIGHWAY by Randal Myler and Mark Harelik.** The story of the beloved and volatile country-music legend Hank Williams, featuring twenty-five of his most unforgettable songs. "[LOST HIGHWAY has] the exhilarating feeling of Williams on stage in a particular place on a particular night…serves up classic country with the edges raw and the energy hot…By the end of the play, you've traveled on a profound emotional journey: LOST HIGHWAY transports its audience and communicates the inspiring message of the beauty and richness of Williams' songs…forceful, clear-eyed, moving, impressive." *–Rolling Stone.* "…honors a very particular musical talent with care and energy… smart, sweet, poignant." *–NY Times.* [7M, 3W] ISBN: 0-8222-1985-9

★ **THE STORY by Tracey Scott Wilson.** An ambitious black newspaper reporter goes against her editor to investigate a murder and finds the *best* story…but at what cost? "A singular new voice…deeply emotional, deeply intellectual, and deeply musical…" *–The New Yorker.* "…a conscientious and absorbing new drama…" *–NY Times.* "…a riveting, tough-minded drama about race, reporting and the truth…" *–A.P.* "… a stylish, attention-holding script that ends on a chilling note that will leave viewers with much to talk about." *–Curtain Up.* [2M, 7W (doubling, flexible casting)] ISBN: 0-8222-1998-0

★ **OUR LADY OF 121st STREET by Stephen Adly Guirgis.** The body of Sister Rose, beloved Harlem nun, has been stolen, reuniting a group of life-challenged childhood friends who square off as they wait for her return. "A scorching and dark new comedy… Mr. Guirgis has one of the finest imaginations for dialogue to come along in years." *–NY Times.* "Stephen Guirgis may be the best playwright in America under forty." *–NY Magazine.* [8M, 4W] ISBN: 0-8222-1965-4

★ **HOLLYWOOD ARMS by Carrie Hamilton and Carol Burnett.** The coming-of-age story of a dreamer who manages to escape her bleak life and follow her romantic ambitions to stardom. Based on Carol Burnett's bestselling autobiography, *One More Time.* "…pure theatre and pure entertainment…" *–Talkin' Broadway.* "…a warm, fuzzy evening of theatre." *–BrodwayBeat.com.* "…chuckles and smiles of recognition or surprise flow naturally…a remarkable slice of life." *–TheatreScene.net.* [5M, 5W, 1 girl] ISBN: 0-8222-1959-X

★ **INVENTING VAN GOGH by Steven Dietz.** A haunting and hallucinatory drama about the making of art, the obsession to create and the fine line that separates truth from myth. "Like a van Gogh painting, Dietz's story is a gorgeous example of excess—one that remakes reality with broad, well-chosen brush strokes. At evening's end, we're left with the author's resounding opinions on art and artifice, and provoked by his constant query into which is greater: van Gogh's art or his violent myth." *–Phoenix New Times.* "Dietz's writing is never simple. It is always brilliant. Shaded, compressed, direct, lucid—he frames his subject with a remarkable understanding of painting as a physical experience." *–Tucson Citizen.* [4M, 1W] ISBN: 0-8222-1954-9

DRAMATISTS PLAY SERVICE, INC.
440 Park Avenue South, New York, NY 10016 212-683-8960 Fax 212-213-1539
postmaster@dramatists.com www.dramatists.com

NEW PLAYS

★ **INTIMATE APPAREL by Lynn Nottage.** The moving and lyrical story of a turn-of-the-century black seamstress whose gifted hands and sewing machine are the tools she uses to fashion her dreams from the whole cloth of her life's experiences. "...Nottage's play has a delicacy and eloquence that seem absolutely right for the time she is depicting..." *–NY Daily News*. "...thoughtful, affecting...The play offers poignant commentary on an era when the cut and color of one's dress—and of course, skin—determined whom one could and could not marry, sleep with, even talk to in public." *–Variety*. [2M, 4W] ISBN: 0-8222-2009-1

★ **BROOKLYN BOY by Donald Margulies.** A witty and insightful look at what happens to a writer when his novel hits the bestseller list. "The characters are beautifully drawn, the dialogue sparkles..." *–nytheatre.com*. "Few playwrights have the mastery to smartly investigate so much through a laugh-out-loud comedy that combines the vintage subject matter of successful writer-returning-to-ethnic-roots with the familiar mid-life crisis." *–Show Business Weekly*. [4M, 3W] ISBN: 0-8222-2074-1

★ **CROWNS by Regina Taylor.** Hats become a springboard for an exploration of black history and identity in this celebratory musical play. "Taylor pulls off a Hat Trick: She scores thrice, turning CROWNS into an artful amalgamation of oral history, fashion show, and musical theater..." *–TheatreMania.com*. "...wholly theatrical...Ms. Taylor has created a show that seems to arise out of spontaneous combustion, as if a bevy of department-store customers simultaneously decided to stage a revival meeting in the changing room." *–NY Times*. [1M, 6W (2 musicians)] ISBN: 0-8222-1963-8

★ **EXITS AND ENTRANCES by Athol Fugard.** The story of a relationship between a young playwright on the threshold of his career and an aging actor who has reached the end of his. "[Fugard] can say more with a single line than most playwrights convey in an entire script...Paraphrasing the title, it's safe to say this drama, making its memorable entrance into our consciousness, is unlikely to exit as long as a theater exists for exceptional work." *–Variety*. "A thought-provoking, elegant and engrossing new play..." *–Hollywood Reporter*. [2M] ISBN: 0-8222-2041-5

★ **BUG by Tracy Letts.** A thriller featuring a pair of star-crossed lovers in an Oklahoma City motel facing a bug invasion, paranoia, conspiracy theories and twisted psychological motives. "...obscenely exciting...top-flight craftsmanship. Buckle up and brace yourself..." *–NY Times*. "...[a] thoroughly outrageous and thoroughly entertaining play...the possibility of enemies, real and imagined, to squash has never been more theatrical." *–A.P.* [3M, 2W] ISBN: 0-8222-2016-4

★ **THOM PAIN (BASED ON NOTHING) by Will Eno.** An ordinary man muses on childhood, yearning, disappointment and loss, as he draws the audience into his last-ditch plea for empathy and enlightenment. "It's one of those treasured nights in the theater—treasured nights anywhere, for that matter—that can leave you both breathless with exhilaration and...in a puddle of tears." *–NY Times*. "Eno's words...are familiar, but proffered in a way that is constantly contradictory to our expectations. Beckett is certainly among his literary ancestors." *–nytheatre.com*. [1M] ISBN: 0-8222-2076-8

★ **THE LONG CHRISTMAS RIDE HOME by Paula Vogel.** Past, present and future collide on a snowy Christmas Eve for a troubled family of five. "...[a] lovely and hauntingly original family drama...a work that breathes so much life into the theater." *–Time Out*. "...[a] delicate visual feast..." *–NY Times*. "...brutal and lovely...the overall effect is magical." *–NY Newsday*. [3M, 3W] ISBN: 0-8222-2003-2

DRAMATISTS PLAY SERVICE, INC.
440 Park Avenue South, New York, NY 10016 212-683-8960 Fax 212-213-1539
postmaster@dramatists.com www.dramatists.com